SIMPLY DELICIOUS 2

By the same author:
Simply Delicious
A Simply Delicious Christmas
Simply Delicious Fish
Simply Delicious in France & Italy
Darina Allen's Simply Delicious Recipes

Darina Allen

SIMPLY

DELICIOUS 2

Published for Radio Telefís Éireann
by
Gill and Macmillan

Published by
Gill and Macmillan Ltd
Goldenbridge
Dublin 8
and
Radio Telefís Éireann
Donnybrook
Dublin 4
© Darina Allen 1990
0 7171 1770 7
Photographs by Des Gaffney and John Rowe, RTE
Food styling by Rory O'Connell
Design by Peter Larrigan
Print origination in Ireland by
Irish Photo Ltd, Dublin and Irish Typesetting and Publishing Ltd, Galway
Printed by Colour Books Ltd, Dublin

A catalogue record is available for this book from the British Library

3 5 7 9 8 6 4

For my father-in-law, Ivan Allen,
and my children,
Isaac, Toby, Lydia and Emily

Contents

The items marked with an asterisk denote recipes which are demonstrated on RTE's *Simply Delicious* television series.

Foreword

After the first *Simply Delicious* programme was shown, a woman stopped me in the street in Cork one day and said: 'You're a great girl, do you know you've got people into the kitchen who never cooked a thing before in their lives!' It was one of the nicest compliments I've ever got, because more than anything else, I want people to discover how easy and enjoyable it can be to cook delicious food—and what a marvellous difference that makes to everyday life! That, once again, is the aim underlying this book and the RTE television series around which it is based. My approach again this time is to introduce to people several basic and extraordinarily useful techniques. Once these have been mastered, you will immediately have an extensive repertoire of recipes at your fingertips, because each one can be used in an infinite number of ways.

To these 'technique' recipes I have added other favourites of mine which suit the *Simply Delicious* theme. Some are fast and filling family stand-bys based on very inexpensive ingredients; others are more sophisticated, a little more costly and perhaps better suited to special occasions—but all are actually easy to make and I promise you they *are* delicious.

Speaking of special occasions, sometimes there is a tendency to make an effort in the kitchen only when guests are invited—condemning the family to do-it-themselves dinners of frozen pies or reheated pizzas, often eaten in relays by people standing at the kitchen counter. There's not a lot of joy in that and still less nutrition. I really do believe that tasty and wholesome food is one of the great anchors of family life, so if you have time, try at least to make the family a nice crusty loaf of brown bread every day. Apart from the fact that good cooking contributes greatly to health and energy, sitting down together to eat and chat is the best recipe I know for cementing relationships. You don't need to use exotic ingredients and you don't need to spend hours in the kitchen—as I think this *Simply Delicious* demonstrates. It's all a matter of deciding to share the pleasure that good simple food brings. But one little word here to the family: be critical of the food you are served if you must, but also make sure to be interested and appreciative. Nobody can cook well and retain their enthusiasm if the audience merely shovels it down and grunts!

My second plea is for people to abandon the idea that entertaining calls for elaborate food. Dinner parties don't have to be grand! It's every bit as enjoyable to have a few friends around for an omelette and salad and good conversation as it is to orchestrate a six-course gourmet menu—far more enjoyable, indeed, since everybody is likely to be more relaxed. All it takes is the confidence to serve something simple.

I hope you will try it right away—along with these *Simply Delicious* recipes.

Acknowledgments

Once again I owe a tremendous debt of gratitude to my mother-in-law, Myrtle Allen, who has taught me so much over the years and who continues to inspire me—a special thank you for giving me permission to reproduce many favourite Ballymaloe recipes. My thanks also to my teachers and assistants at the Ballymaloe Cookery School, Florrie Cullinane, Susie Noriega, Fionnuala Ryan, Barbara Hogan and Greg Dawson for cheerful and unstinting support. A special mention for my brother Rory O'Connell, whose inspired food-styling makes our food come to life on the page, and for Des Gaffney and John Roe for the care and tremendous expertise they brought to the photographs.

A special thank you to the RTE crews who have held my hand and mopped my brow through the making of two television programme series. I want to mention each of them by name because they each have a special place in my heart—Clare Duignan, who produced the first of the two 'Simply Delicious' series and Colette Farmer, who directed both—two very professional ladies of tremendous ability. Roy Bedell, who shot the first series and was joined by cameraman Ken Fogarty in the second series. Soundmen Pat Johns and Michael Cassidy, who kept my mind off the pressure with endless jokes and gags. Sean Keville, the 'sparks', who provided the 'high lights' on both occasions—my flashing glasses and bobbing head certainly presented him with a challenge. And last, but certainly not least, two remarkable production assistants, Patricia Swan and Kevin Cummins, who had the unenviable task of keeping track of continuity on a cookery programme—believe me, that's the sort of stuff that nightmares are made of. Each and every one of them had more faith in me than I had in myself and so I was challenged to live up to their expectations. I hope that I did in some measure, they certainly deserve it—a very sincere thank you to them all.

A very special mention too for my secretaries, Rosalie Dunne and Adrienne Morrissey, who typed the manuscript and often helped me late into the night. A special thanks must also go to my publishers, Gill and Macmillan, and in particular D Rennison-Kunz, Mary Kinsella and Mary Dowey—I could not possibly have written three books within one year without their tremendous help and support. And last, but not least, a big thank you to my husband, Tim.

Glossary

Arachide oil: Peanut or groundnut oil

Bain-marie (or water bath): Can be any deep container, half-filled with hot water, in which delicate foods, e.g. custards or fish mousses are cooked in their moulds or terrines. The bain-marie is put into a low or moderate oven and the food is protected from direct heat by the gentle, steamy atmosphere, without risk of curdling. The term bain-marie is also used for a similar container which will hold several pans to keep soups, vegetables or stews warm during restaurant service.

Bouquet garni: A small bunch of fresh herbs used to flavour stews, casseroles, stocks or soups, usually consisting of parsley stalks, a sprig of thyme, perhaps a bay leaf and an outside stalk of celery. Remove before serving.

Concassé: Concassé means roughly chopped, usually applied to tomatoes. Pour boiling water over the firm, very ripe tomatoes, leave for 10 seconds, then pour off the water. Peel off the skin, cut in half, remove the seeds with a teaspoon or melon-baller, cut in quarters and chop into $\frac{1}{4}$ inch (5 mm) or $\frac{1}{8}$ inch (3 mm) dice. Concassé may be added to a sauce or used as a garnish.

De-glaze: After meat has been sautéed or roasted, the pan or roasting dish is de-greased and then a liquid is poured into the pan to dissolve the coagulated and caramelised pan juices. This is the basis of many sauces and gravies. The liquid could be water, stock or alcohol, e.g. wine or brandy.

De-grease: To remove surplus fat from a liquid or a pan, either by pouring off or by skimming the surface with a spoon.

Egg wash: A raw egg beaten with a pinch of salt; it is brushed on raw tarts, pies, buns and biscuits to give them a shiny, golden glaze when cooked.

Grill pan: A heavy cast-iron pan, with a ridged bottom, either rounded or rectangular. The ridges mark the food attractively while keeping the meat or fish from direct contact with the fat. A heavy pan gives a good even heat.

Lardons: A French term for narrow strips of streaky bacon

xv

Macerate: To soak fruit in syrup or other liquid so that it will absorb the flavour and in some cases become more tender.

Paper lid: When we are sweating vegetables for the base of a soup or stew, we quite often cover them with a butter wrapper or a lid made from greaseproof paper which fits the saucepan exactly. This keeps in the steam and helps to sweat the vegetables.

Ramekins: Little dishes, usually made of pottery or china, approximately 3 inches (7.5 cm) in diameter and 2 inches (5 cm) deep.

Reduce: To boil down a liquid to concentrate the flavour. This is a very important technique in sauce-making.

Roux: Equal quantities of butter and flour cooked together for 2 minutes over a gentle heat. This mixture may be whisked into boiling liquid to thicken, e.g. gravies, sauces, milk etc.

Silicone paper: A non-stick parchment paper which is widely used for lining baking trays, cake tins etc. It may be used several times over and is particularly useful when making meringues or chocolates, because they simply peel off the paper. 'Bakewell' is the brand name; it is available in most supermarkets and newsagents.

(To) Sponge: A term used when working with powdered gelatine. The gelatine is sprinkled over a specified amount of liquid and left to sit for 4–5 minutes. During this period, the gelatine soaks up the water and becomes 'spongy' in texture—hence the name. Gelatine is easier to dissolve if it is sponged before melting.

Sweat: To cook vegetables in a little fat or oil over a gentle heat in a covered saucepan, until they are almost soft but not coloured.

Soups and Starters

If you have my other books you'll know by now that I consider soup to be one of the greatest mainstays any cook can master. It's heartwarming and wholesome and absolutely central to my philosophy that even the simplest food to prepare can also taste delicious! Soup can adapt itself to every occasion. Obviously it can be the first course of a dinner or a quick and nourishing lunchtime or after-school snack, but there's no doubt about it that a good home-made soup served with crusty brown bread and a green salad is a meal fit for a king.

There is one point I'd like to make, however: I'm not at all sure that I agree with people who feel that soup is a handy way of using up old vegetables and other left-overs. That seems to me to be a slightly hit and miss approach which can sometimes have delicious results but more often than not can be responsible for turning your entire family off 'soup' altogether, so for best results I suggest you use good ingredients and tried-and-tested recipes.

First comes Mushroom Soup, an all-time favourite which appeals to both the simple and the sophisticated palate. It is the fastest of all the soups to make: just about 20 minutes from start to finish. It is also the exception that proves the rule about using vegetables in their prime, because this recipe actually tastes better if you use mushrooms which are a few days old—handy if you have forgotten a bag of them at the bottom of the fridge, or if you have access to flat or wild mushrooms they are even better. As I write, the fields around my house are white with wild mushrooms and there is even an occasional mushroom on the lawn! In a situation of surplus like this, the great advantage of this recipe is that you can simply make and freeze the mushroom base and then add stock when you want to serve it.

For something slightly more unusual but equally tasty, I hope you will try Watercress Soup. The main ingredient is another wonderful free food for country-dwellers (just make sure you pick it in streams of clean and constantly moving water)—and luckily watercress is now becoming more widely available in shops, too. This soup should be a fresh green colour and is full of vitamins and minerals.

Last, but certainly not least, of the soups, since they are among the most substantial, are Celery and Lovage Soup (in which lovage contributes to the strong celery flavour but is not essential) and Potato

1

and Smoky Bacon Soup, a recipe using two quintessentially Irish ingredients which was actually given to me by a German friend, Else Schiller. It was a favourite recipe in the Schleswig-Holstein area, where Else comes from.

For a light first course, I'm particularly fond of the Salades Tièdes — warm salads which to my mind are one of the most valuable parts of the legacy of *nouvelle cuisine*, the French food fashion of the eighties. Apart from Salade Tiède with Chicken Livers, Bacon and Croûtons, I have included several mouthwatering examples to show how easy it is to invent your own combination of ingredients for these light little starter salads, in which an interesting variety of cold salad leaves is topped with something tasty, hot from the pan. Their success depends upon the contrast of flavour and texture — hot *v* cold, soft *v* crisp, sharp *v* mild. There is plenty of scope to experiment with dressings, too, using different oils and vinegars. For example, you can use walnut and hazelnut oil as well as virgin olive oil, and sherry, balsamic and champagne vinegars as well as the more ordinary red and white vinegars. All you need is plenty of imagination and a measure of restraint! Don't lose the run of yourself and remember to concentrate on the flavour: they should taste as stunning as they look.

There's also a fruity starter, Orange, Mint and Grapefruit Cocktail; an Avocado Mousse with Tomato and Basil Salad, which uses the technique for gelatine demonstrated in the series in a delightful savoury way; and some lovely first courses are included for fish lovers. First among them is the best recipe I have ever tasted for Ceviche, given to me by my Peruvian cook assistant, Susie Noriega. Until recently I think most people would have been appalled at the idea of being presented with what would appear to be virtually raw fish as the prelude to a dinner. However, fear not, the fish in Ceviche is actually slowly and splendidly 'cooked' by the action of the lime juice.

Oeufs Mimosa is a pretty variation of Egg Mayonnaise, in which a prawn is hidden as a surprise inside the shell of each hard-boiled egg half, covered with home-made mayonnaise and decorated with sieved egg yolk. Compare that with the hard-boiled egg and bottled salad cream that passes for egg mayonnaise in many places!

And so to prawns, the best loved seafood luxury of all. Wonderful fresh, fat Dublin Bay prawns are such a treat that they deserve special care. Buttery Bretonne Sauce with fresh herbs and green Maille mustard is one solution which can also transform many lesser fish into a feast.

A word of advice about the prawns you buy. In my experience, there is no such thing as a bargain: all the good ones are expensive, and the bigger they are, the better they will be to eat. If you find you have to use frozen prawns, the same rule applies. Beware the suspiciously cheap ones that look large and smooth. The trick that has been used here is to dip them in water and freeze them several times over, to add to their bulk. Don't fall for it! After defrosting, all that is left is a pool of salty water and miserable specimens in a mushy pile.

The fastest fish starter comes last. Smoked Trout with Cucumber and Horseradish Sauce takes only the few minutes required to grate fresh horseradish into a simple sauce and open a vacuum pack of tender, moist warm-smoked Irish trout, which is easy to find these days. Like the trout, fresh horseradish should be easy to track down. As it's useful in other ways and obligatory with roast beef, you may even decide to grow it if you have room in your garden for its expansion. In no time at all you'll have enough to supply your entire neighbourhood!

One of the great secrets is not to overdo things. If your first course is fairly substantial, serve small quantities and balance it with a lighter main course—and vice versa. People can just as easily feel hung over from having too much food as too much drink!

Mushroom Soup*

Serves 8–9

Many people have forgotten how delicious a home-made mushroom soup can be; it's one of the fastest of all soups to make and surely everyone's favourite. Mushroom Soup is best made with flat mushrooms or button mushrooms a few days old, which have developed a slightly stronger flavour.

2 ozs (55 g/$\frac{1}{2}$ stick) butter
1 oz (30 g/scant $\frac{1}{4}$ cup) flour
4 ozs (110 g/1 cup) very finely chopped onion
1 lb (450 g/5 cups) mushrooms, very finely chopped

salt and freshly ground pepper
1 pint (600 ml/2$\frac{1}{2}$ cups) milk
1 pint (600 ml/2$\frac{1}{2}$ cups) home-made chicken stock
(*Simply Delicious*, **page 35**)

Chop the onion finely. Melt the butter in a saucepan on a gentle heat. Toss the onions in it, cover and sweat until soft and completely cooked. Meanwhile, chop up the mushrooms very finely. Add to the saucepan and cook for a further 3 or 4 minutes. Now stir in the flour, cook on a low heat for 2–3 minutes, season with salt and freshly ground pepper, then add the stock and milk gradually, stirring all the time; increase the heat and bring to the boil. Taste and add a dash of cream if necessary.

Wild Mushroom Soup

Every few years after a good warm summer, lots of wild mushrooms (*Agaricus Campestris*) appear in the old meadows. Make them into a soup using the above recipe. If you have a surplus of wild mushrooms, just make the base of the soup, but don't add the stock or milk; this purée may be frozen and turned into a soup as you need it.

Watercress Soup

Serves 6–8

1$\frac{1}{2}$ ozs (45 g/generous $\frac{1}{4}$ stick) butter
4 ozs (110 g/1 cup) chopped onions
5 ozs (140 g/1 cup) chopped potatoes
8 ozs (225 g/5 cups) chopped watercress

1 pint (600 ml/2$\frac{1}{2}$ cups) water *or* light home-made chicken stock (*Simply Delicious*, **page 35**)
1 pint (600 ml/2$\frac{1}{2}$ cups) creamy milk
salt and freshly ground pepper

Garnish
2 tablesp. ($\frac{1}{8}$ cup) whipped
cream (optional)

watercress leaves

Melt the butter in a heavy-bottomed saucepan. When it foams, add the potatoes and onions and toss them until well coated. Sprinkle with salt and freshly ground pepper. Cover and sweat on a gentle heat for 10 minutes. Add the stock and milk, bring to the boil and cook until the potatoes and onions are soft. Add the watercress and boil *with the lid off* for 4–5 minutes approx. until the watercress is cooked. Do not overcook or the soup will lose its fresh green colour. Purée the soup in a liquidiser or food processor. Taste and correct seasoning.

Serve in warm bowls garnished with a blob of whipped cream and a watercress leaf.

Celery and Lovage Soup

Serves 6–8

Lovage is a perennial herb with a pronounced celery flavour. Use it sparingly to enhance the flavour of soups, stews and stocks.

1$\frac{1}{2}$ ozs (45 g/generous $\frac{1}{4}$ stick)
butter
4 ozs (110 g/1 cup) chopped
onions
5 ozs (140 g/1 cup) chopped
potatoes
1 lb (450 g/4 cups) finely
chopped celery

1 sprig of lovage (optional)
2 pints (1.1 L/5 cups) light home-
made chicken stock (*Simply*
***Delicious*, page 35)**
salt and freshly ground pepper
a little cream *or* creamy milk

Melt the butter in a heavy-bottomed saucepan. When it foams, add the potatoes, onions, celery and lovage; toss in the butter until evenly coated. Season with salt and freshly ground pepper. Cover with a paper lid (to keep in the steam) and the saucepan lid and sweat over a gentle heat for 10 minutes approx., until the vegetables are soft but not coloured. Add the chicken stock and simmer until the celery is fully cooked, 10–12 minutes approx. Liquidise the soup; add a little more stock or creamy milk to thin to the required consistency. Taste and correct the seasoning.

Potato and Smoky Bacon Soup

Serves 8–9

A wonderfully warming winter soup—almost a meal in itself.

5 ozs (150 g) smoked streaky
  bacon
10 ozs (300 g/2½ cups) finely
  chopped onions
1 oz (30 g/¼ stick) butter
2 tablesp. (⅛ cup) oil
1 lb 2 ozs (500 g) potatoes

1 pint (600 ml/2½ cups) home-
  made chicken stock (*Simply
  Delicious*, page 35)
salt and freshly ground pepper
1 pint (600 ml/2½ cups) milk
1 tablesp. chopped parsley

Remove the rind from the bacon and keep aside. Chop the smoky bacon and onions very finely. Melt the butter and oil in a saucepan, add the bacon and cook for a few minutes, then add the onions; cover and sweat on a gentle heat until soft but not coloured. Add the stock and leave to simmer while you prepare the potatoes. Add the bacon rind to the stock. Peel the potatoes and chop very finely, add to the saucepan and stir until it becomes quite thick and sticky. Season with freshly ground pepper and a little salt (watch the salt because of the bacon). Keep on stirring and add the milk slowly. Boil until the potatoes are soft—they will disintegrate into a purée. Remove the bacon rind, add the chopped parsley, taste and serve. Add a little more chicken stock or milk if the soup is too thick.

Salade Tiède with Chicken Livers, Bacon and Croûtons*

Serves 4

a selection of lettuces and salad
  leaves, e.g. butterhead,
  iceberg, lollo rosso, frisée and
  golden marjoram
8 nasturtium flowers (optional)
6 fresh chicken livers

4 ozs (110 g) streaky bacon, cut
  into ¼ inch (5 mm) lardons (see
  glossary)
12 tiny croûtons of white bread
salt and freshly ground pepper

Dressing
1 tablesp. red wine vinegar
3 tablesp. olive oil *or* 1½ tablesp.
  olive oil and

1½ tablesp. sunflower oil
a small clove of garlic mashed
2 teasp. chopped parsley

First make the croûtons. If you can find a very thin French stick, cut $\frac{1}{4}$ inch (5 mm) slices off that; alternatively, stamp out slices in rounds from a slice of white bread with a biscuit cutter $1\frac{1}{2}$ inches (4 cm) wide. Then spread a little butter on each side and bake in a moderate oven, 180°C/350°F/regulo 4, for 20 minutes approx. or until golden on both sides; it may be necessary to turn them half way through cooking. Drain on kitchen paper and keep warm (croûtons could be prepared ahead and reheated later).

Next make the Dressing by whisking all the ingredients together. Remove the rind from the bacon and cut into $\frac{1}{4}$ inch (5 mm) lardons; blanch, refresh in cold water, drain and dry on kitchen paper. Wash and dry the salad leaves and tear into bite-sized bits. Wash and dry the chicken livers and divide each liver into 2 pieces. Just before serving, heat a dash of oil in a frying pan and sauté the lardons of bacon until crisp and golden.

To serve: Shake the Dressing and toss the salad leaves in just enough Dressing to make them glisten. Divide between 4 plates making sure that there is some height in the centre; it should look as though it has been dropped onto the plate, but if it doesn't drop reasonably attractively you could rearrange the leaves slightly. Scatter the hot bacon over the salad, season the chicken livers and cook gently in the bacon fat for just a few minutes. I like them slightly pink in the centre, but if you want them better done, cook for a minute or two longer. Arrange 3 pieces around the top of each salad, put 3 croûtons on each plate, garnish with a few nasturtium flowers for extra 'posh' and peppery taste and serve immediately.

Salade Tiède with Avocado, Bacon and Walnut Oil Dressing

Serves 6

a selection of lettuces and salad leaves, e.g. butterhead, iceberg, endive, raddichio trevisano, watercress, salad burnet, tiny spring onions etc.—the larger the selection the more interesting the salad will be

6 ozs (170 g) streaky bacon, in the piece, green *or* lightly smoked
4 slices of white bread
1 large *or* 2 small avocados

Walnut Oil Dressing
4 tablesp. ($\frac{1}{4}$ cup) walnut oil *or* **2
tablesp. ($\frac{1}{8}$ cup) each walnut oil
and sunflower** *or* **arachide oil
mixed**
**1 tablesp. and 1 teasp. wine
vinegar**

1 teasp. chopped chives
1 teasp. chopped parsley
salt and freshly ground pepper

Garnish
18 walnut halves

Wash and dry the salad leaves and tear them into bite-sized pieces. Put
into a bowl, cover and refrigerate until needed. Cut the rind off the
piece of bacon and discard. Cut the bacon into $\frac{1}{4}$ inch (5 mm) lardons
and then blanch and refresh in cold water if necessary. Dry on kitchen
paper. Cut the crusts off the bread and cut into exact $\frac{1}{4}$ inch (5 mm)
cubes. Fry until golden in clarified butter (see page 16) or a mixture of
butter and oil. Drain on kitchen paper. Make the Walnut Oil Dressing
in the usual way by whisking the ingredients together; add the
chopped herbs. Halve the avocado, remove the stone, peel and cut
into $\frac{1}{2}$ inch (1 cm) dice.

To serve: Toss the salad in just enough Dressing to make the leaves
glisten. Add the crisp, warm croûtons and the diced avocado. Toss
gently and divide the salad between 6 plates. Fry the bacon in a little
olive oil in a hot pan until crisp and golden, then scatter the *hot* bacon
over the salad. Garnish with a few walnut halves. Serve immediately.

A Warm Salad of Mussels
with Tomato Concassé and Watercress

Serves 4

**a selection of as many types of
lettuces and salad leaves as are
available, e.g. iceberg, endive,
rocket, oakleaf and butterhead**
watercress for garnishing
**1 tomato, peeled, seeded and
flesh cut into $\frac{1}{4}$ inch (5 mm)
dice (concassé)**

**salt, freshly ground pepper and
sugar**
2 scallions, cut at an angle
24 mussels
1 avocado

French Dressing
1 tablesp. wine vinegar
2 tablesp. ($\frac{1}{8}$ cup) sunflower oil *or*
  arachide oil
1 tablesp. virgin olive oil
a small clove of garlic (made into
  a paste)

1 tiny spring onion *or* scallion
  finely chopped
a teasp. of finely chopped
  parsley
a pinch of mustard
salt and freshly ground pepper

Liquidise or whisk the above ingredients for French Dressing.

Wash and dry the required amount of salad leaves and tear into bite-sized pieces. Season the tomato concassé with salt, freshly ground pepper and sugar. Cut the scallions, both green and white parts, into slices at an angle. Wash the mussels well, put them into a heavy frying pan in a single layer, cover with a folded tea-towel and place on a low heat. As soon as the shells start to open, lift them from the pan, take the mussels from their shells and remove the beard as you do so.

Halve and peel the avocado, remove the stone, cut the flesh into $\frac{1}{4}$ inch (5 mm) dice and season with salt and freshly ground pepper. Just before serving, toss the salad leaves gently with French Dressing—just enough to make the leaves glisten. Arrange the salad on 4 white plates, heaping it slightly in the centre. Arrange the warm mussels and avocado on the salad as appetisingly as possible. Sprinkle with tomato concassé and sliced scallions. Garnish with sprigs of watercress and serve immediately.

A Warm Salad with Irish Blue Cheese

Serves 4

Some ripe, crumbly Cashel Blue cheese—made in Fethard, Co. Tipperary by Jane and Louis Grubb—would be wonderful for this salad.

a selection of lettuces and salad
  leaves, e.g. iceberg, endive,
  rocket, oakleaf and butterhead
12 round croûtons $\frac{1}{4}$ inch (5 mm)
  thick of bread, cut from a thin
  French stick
1$\frac{1}{2}$ ozs (45 g/generous $\frac{1}{4}$ stick) soft
  butter

a clove of garlic, peeled
5 ozs (140 g) smoked streaky
  bacon, cut into $\frac{1}{4}$ inch (5 mm)
  lardons
2 ozs (55 g) Cashel Blue cheese

Vinaigrette Dressing
1 tablesp. balsamic vinegar *or*
  sherry vinegar *or* **red wine**
  vinegar
1 tablesp. arachide *or* **sunflower**
  oil

2 tablesp. olive oil
salt and freshly ground pepper
2 teasp. chopped chervil and 2
  teasp. chopped tarragon *or* **4**
  teasp. chopped parsley

Garnish
1 heaped tablesp. sprigs of
  chervil *or* **freshly chopped**
  parsley

Whisk the above ingredients together for Vinaigrette Dressing.

Wash and dry the mixture of lettuces and salad leaves and tear into bite-sized pieces. Spread both sides of the rounds of bread with softened butter. Put onto a baking sheet and bake in a moderate oven, 180°C/350°F/regulo 4, until golden and crisp on both sides, 20 minutes approx. Rub them with a cut clove of garlic and keep hot in a low oven with the door slightly open. Blanch and refresh the bacon, dry well on kitchen paper. Just before serving, sauté the bacon dice in a little olive oil until golden.

To serve: Dress the lettuces with some vinaigrette in a salad bowl. Use just enough to make the leaves glisten. Crumble the cheese with a fork and add it to the salad, tossing them well together. Divide between 4 plates. Scatter the *hot* crispy bacon over the top, put 3 warm croûtons on each plate and sprinkle sprigs of chervil or chopped parsley over the salad. Serve immediately.

A Warm Salad of Goat's Cheese with Walnut Oil Dressing

Serves 6

1 fresh, soft goat's cheese, e.g.
  Cléire, Lough Caum *or* **St Tola**
6 slices toasted French bread
18–24 fresh walnuts

a selection of lettuces and salad
  leaves, e.g. butterhead, frisée,
  oakleaf, raddichio trevisano,
  rocket, salad burnet, golden
  marjoram, and chive *or* **wild**
  garlic flowers to garnish

Walnut Oil Dressing
2 tablesp. white wine vinegar
4 tablesp. walnut oil

2 tablesp. sunflower *or* **arachide**
  oil
salt and freshly ground pepper

Wash and dry the salad leaves and tear all the large leaves into bite-sized bits. Make the Dressing by whisking all the ingredients together. Cover each piece of toasted French bread with a three-quarter-inch (2 cm) slice of goat's cheese. Just before serving, preheat the grill. Place the slices of bread and cheese under the grill and toast for 5 or 6 minutes or until the cheese is soft and slightly golden.

Meanwhile, toss the salad greens lightly in the Walnut Oil Dressing and drop a small handful onto each plate. Place a hot goat's cheese croûton in the centre of each salad, scatter with a few walnut pieces and serve immediately. We sprinkle wild garlic or chive flowers over the salad in season.

Note: This salad may be used either as a starter or as a cheese course.

A Warm Winter Salad with Duck Livers and Hazelnut Oil Dressing

Serves 4

6 fresh duck livers *or*, if
    unavailable, chicken livers
½ oz (15 g/1 tablesp.) butter
12 chicory leaves
2 ozs (55g/½ cup) grated celeriac
2 ozs (55g/½ cup) grated carrot

4 leaves of butterhead lettuce
4 sprigs of watercress
2 large leaves of iceberg lettuce
4 leaves of raddichio trevisano *or*
    4 leaves of oakleaf lettuce

Hazelnut Oil Dressing
6 tablesp. hazelnut oil
2 tablesp. (⅛ cup) wine vinegar

salt and freshly ground pepper

Garnish
1 tablesp. chopped chives

Wash and dry the salad leaves and tear them into bite-sized pieces. Whisk together the ingredients for the Dressing. Grate the carrot and celeriac on the large part of the grater and toss in 3 tablespoons approx. of Dressing. Taste and season with salt and freshly ground pepper if necessary. Toss the salad leaves in a little more of the Dressing—just enough to make the leaves glisten.

Melt the butter in a sauté pan, season the livers and cook over a gentle heat. While the livers are cooking, arrange 3 leaves of chicory in a star shape on each plate. Put a mound of salad leaves in the centre with some celeriac and carrot on top. Finally, cut the livers in half and while still warm arrange 3 pieces on each salad. Sprinkle with chopped chives and serve immediately.

Orange, Mint and Grapefruit Cocktail

Serves 4

2 grapefruit
2 oranges

2 tablesp. freshly chopped mint
1 tablesp. sugar approx.

Garnish
4 sprigs of fresh mint

Peel and carefully segment the oranges and grapefruit into a bowl. Add the sugar and chopped mint; taste and add more sugar if necessary. Chill. Serve in pretty little bowls or, alternatively, arrange the segments of orange and grapefruit alternately on the plate in a circle; pour a little juice over the fruit. Garnish with a sprig of fresh mint.

Avocado Mousse with Tomato and Basil Salad

Serves 6

This is a good way of using up avocados which may be a little too soft to prepare in the usual way.

2 ripe avocados
$\frac{1}{4}$ teasp. grated onion
2 fl ozs (50 ml/$\frac{1}{4}$ cup) chicken
   stock (*Simply Delicious*, **page 35**)

2 tablesp. ($\frac{1}{8}$ cup) French dressing
   (see Billy's French Dressing,
   Simply Delicious, **page 57**)
2 teasp. lemon juice
$\frac{1}{4}$ teasp. salt
$\frac{1}{4}$ oz (2 rounded teasp.) gelatine

Garnish
sprigs of fresh basil, chervil *or*
   lemon balm

6 round moulds, $2\frac{1}{2}$ × $1\frac{1}{2}$ inches
   (6.5 × 4 cm); $2\frac{1}{2}$ fl ozs
   (generous 50 ml) capacity,
   brushed with a light oil, e.g.
   arachide

12

Peel and stone the avocados. Liquidise the first six ingredients together, taste and season. For every $\frac{3}{4}$ pint (15 fl ozs/450 ml) use $\frac{1}{4}$ oz (2 rounded teasp.) of gelatine and 2 tablespoons of water. Sponge the gelatine in the cold water; place the bowl in a pan of simmering water until the gelatine has completely dissolved. Add a little of the avocado mixture to the gelatine, stir well and then combine with the remainder of the avocado purée. Stir well again. Pour into the prepared moulds and leave to set for 4 or 5 hours.

To serve: Place an Avocado Mousse in the centre of a white plate and garnish with a ring of Tomato Salad and some sprigs of basil, chervil or lemon balm.

Note: If the avocado purée does not measure $\frac{3}{4}$ pint, make up with one tablesp. or more of whipped cream.

Tomato and Basil Salad

6 very ripe, firm tomatoes
1 teasp. chopped fresh basil *or*
mint
salt and freshly ground pepper
and sugar

French Dressing (see Billy's
French Dressing, *Simply*
Delicious, **page 57)**

Slice the tomatoes into 3 or 4 rounds around the centre. Arrange in a single layer on a flat plate. Sprinkle with salt, sugar and several grinds of pepper. Toss immediately in just enough French Dressing to coat, and sprinkle with chopped mint or basil. Taste for seasoning. Tomatoes must be dressed immediately they are cut to seal in their flavour.

Susie Noriega's Peruvian Ceviche

Serves 10–12 as a starter

2 lbs (900g) fillets of very fresh
white fish, monkfish, cod *or*
plaice
2 cloves of finely chopped garlic
1–2 fresh chillies
4 limes

2 lemons
3 ozs (85 g/scant 1 cup) finely
sliced onions
fresh coriander
salt and freshly ground pepper

Garnish
crisp lettuce leaves
5–6 spring onions
sweetcorn

1 green pepper and 1 red pepper,
finely diced
2 avocados

Skin the fish; slice or cube into $\frac{1}{2}$ inch (1 cm) pieces and put it into a deep stainless steel or china bowl. Squeeze the juice from the lemons and limes and pour over the fish. Sprinkle with salt, freshly ground pepper and chopped garlic. Cover and leave to marinate for 3 or 4 hours in a fridge. Next add the fresh coriander, sliced onions and chillies and half of the finely diced red and green peppers. Cover and leave for $2\frac{1}{2}$ hours in the fridge. Then serve or keep covered until later.

To serve: Arrange a few crisp lettuce leaves on a plate and place a tablespoon of Ceviche in the centre. Decorate with slices of avocado, diced peppers, sweetcorn and spring onions. Serve it with crusty white bread.

Oeufs Mimosa

Serves 4

Oeufs Mimosa may be served on a cold buffet, but be sure to garnish with prawns or shrimps in case anyone is allergic to shellfish.

4 eggs (preferably free-range)	$\frac{1}{4}$ pint (150 ml/generous $\frac{1}{2}$ cup)
8 cooked prawns	home-made mayonnaise (see
or 16 shrimps	page 15)
salt and freshly ground pepper	a few lettuce leaves

Garnish
**sprigs of watercress, a few whole
shrimps or prawns**

Bring a small saucepan of water to the boil; lower the eggs gradually into the water one by one, bring the water back to the boil and cook for 10 minutes; pour off the water and cover the eggs with cold water. When cold, shell and cut in half lengthways. Sieve the yolks, reserve a little for garnish, mix the remainder with 3–4 tablespoons of home-made mayonnaise and taste for seasoning.

Put 1 or 2 cooked shrimps or prawns into each egg white and spoon some egg mayonnaise mixture into each one; round off the top to look like whole eggs. Then thin the remaining mayonnaise with hot water to coating consistency and coat the eggs carefully. Sprinkle with the reserved egg yolk.

Serve on a bed of lettuces and garnish with sprigs of watercress and a few whole shrimps or prawns.

Prawns on Brown Bread with Mayonnaise

Serves 4

Don't dismiss this very simple starter. Prawns are wonderful served on good, fresh bread with a home-made Mayonnaise.

6 ozs (170 g) freshly cooked
   prawns *or* shrimps
4–8 leaves butterhead *or* oakleaf
   or lollo rosso lettuce
3–4 tablesp. home-made
   Mayonnaise

4 slices of buttered Ballymaloe
   brown yeast bread (*Simply
   Delicious*, **page 74**)

Garnish
sprigs of watercress, flat parsley,
   fennel *or* garden cress

4 segments of lemon

Put a slice of buttered bread on a plate, arrange 1 or 2 lettuce leaves on top and place 5–6 fat, freshly cooked prawns on the lettuce. Pipe a coil of home-made Mayonnaise on the prawns. Garnish with lemon wedges and sprigs of watercress, flat parsley, fennel or garden cress.

Note: If using shrimps, use a little of the coral for garnish.

Mayonnaise

2 egg yolks (preferably
   free-range)
$\frac{1}{4}$ teasp. salt
a pinch of English mustard *or* $\frac{1}{4}$
   teasp. French mustard

1 tablesp. (15 ml) white wine
   vinegar
8 fl ozs (250 ml/1 cup) oil
   (sunflower, arachide *or* olive
   oil, *or* a mixture)

Put the egg yolks into a bowl with the mustard, salt and 1 dessert-spoon of wine vinegar (keep the whites to make meringues). Put the oil into a measure. Take a whisk in one hand and oil in the other and drip the oil onto the egg yolks, drop by drop, whisking at the same time. Within a minute you will notice that the mixture is beginning to thicken. When this happens you can add the oil a little faster, but don't get too cheeky or it will suddenly curdle because the egg yolks can only absorb the oil at a certain pace. When all the oil has been added, whisk in the remaining vinegar. Taste and add a little more seasoning if necessary.

If the Mayonnaise curdles it will suddenly become quite thin, and, if left sitting, the oil will start to float to the top of the sauce. If this happens you can quite easily rectify the situation by putting another egg yolk or 1–2 tablespoons of boiling water into a clean bowl, then whisk in the curdled Mayonnaise, a half teaspoon at a time until it emulsifies again.

Prawn and Basil Pâté

Serves 6

This delicious little pâté is particularly good for using up a few leftovers or soft prawns.

8 ozs (225 g/1½ cups) cooked, peeled prawns *or* shrimps
4 tablesp. (¼ cup) olive oil
a dash of cayenne pepper

juice of 1 lime *or* ½ lemon
4 fresh basil leaves
salt if necessary
Clarified Butter to seal (see below)

Put all the ingredients into a food processor and whizz for a few seconds until they form a paste. Taste for seasoning; it may be necessary to add salt. Pack the mixture into little pots or a terrine. Seal with Clarified Butter. Serve chilled with hot, thin toast.

If you are using freshly boiled prawn tails in the shell, allow 1½ lbs (675 g) approx. gross measure, 3 lbs (1.35 kg) with heads on.

Clarified Butter: Melt 8 ozs (225 g/1 cup) butter gently in a saucepan or in the oven. Allow it to stand for a few minutes, then spoon the crusty white layer of salt particles off the top of the melted butter. Underneath this crust there is clear liquid butter which is called Clarified Butter. The milky liquid at the bottom can be discarded or used in a béchamel sauce.

Clarified Butter is excellent for cooking because it can withstand a higher temperature when the salt particles and milk are removed. It will keep covered in a refrigerator for several weeks.

Buttered Prawns with Bretonne Sauce*

Serves 4 as a starter, 2 as a main course

2 lbs (900 g) whole prawns (yields 6 ozs (170 g) prawn tails approx.)

1 oz (30 g/¼ stick) butter
4 pints (2.3 L/10 cups) water
2 tablesp. salt

16

Mushroom Soup

Salade Tiède with Chicken Livers, Bacon and Croûtons

Monkfish Steamed in its Own Juices with Tomato and Dill

Three-minute Fish

Moules Provençale

Bretonne Sauce

1 egg yolk (preferably
  free-range)
$\frac{1}{2}$ teasp. French mustard (we use
  Maille mustard with green
  herbs)

1 tablesp. mixed finely chopped
  chives, fennel, parsley and
  thyme
3 ozs (85 g/$\frac{3}{4}$ stick) butter

Garnish
flat parsley *or* **fresh fennel**

Bring to the boil 4 pints (2.3 L/10 cups) of water and add 2 tablespoons of salt. De-vein the prawns. Toss them into the boiling water and as soon as the water returns to the boil, test a prawn and then remove immediately. Very large prawns may take $\frac{1}{2}$–1 minute more. Allow to cool and then remove the shells.

Next make the Bretonne Sauce. Whisk the egg yolks with the mustard and herbs in a bowl. Bring the butter to the boil and pour it in a steady stream onto the egg yolks, whisking continuously until the sauce thickens to a light coating consistency as with a Hollandaise. Keep warm in a flask or place in a pottery or plastic bowl (*not* stainless steel) in a saucepan of hot but not boiling water.

Just before serving, toss the prawns in 1 oz (30 g/$\frac{1}{4}$ stick) foaming butter until heated through. Heap them onto a hot serving dish. Coat with Bretonne Sauce. Garnish with flat parsley or fresh fennel and serve immediately.

Smoked Trout with Cucumber Salad and Horseradish Sauce

Serves 8

8 fillets of smoked trout (either
  smoked sea trout *or* rainbow
  trout)
$\frac{1}{2}$ cucumber
salt, freshly ground pepper and
  sugar

1 teasp. chopped fresh fennel *or*
  $\frac{1}{2}$ teasp. chopped fresh dill
a sprinkle of wine vinegar
Horseradish Sauce

Garnish
lemon segments

fresh dill *or* **fennel**

Make the Horseradish Sauce as directed below.

Thinly slice the unpeeled cucumber. Sprinkle with a few drops of vinegar and season with salt, sugar and a little freshly ground pepper. Stir in some finely chopped fennel or dill.

To assemble the salad: Place a fillet of smoked trout on each individual serving plate. Arrange the Cucumber Salad along the side and pipe some fresh Horseradish Sauce on top of the trout. Garnish with a segment of lemon and some fresh herbs.

Horseradish Sauce

This makes a mild Horseradish Sauce; if you would like something that will really clear the sinuses, just increase the quantity of grated horseradish!

8 fl ozs (250 ml/1 cup) softly whipped cream
2 teasp. wine vinegar
1 teasp. lemon juice
$\frac{1}{4}$ teasp. mustard

$\frac{1}{4}$ teasp. salt
a pinch of freshly ground pepper
1 teasp. sugar
$1\frac{1}{2}$ tablesp. grated horseradish

Scrub the horseradish root well, peel and grate. Put the grated horseradish into a bowl with the vinegar, lemon juice, mustard, salt, freshly ground pepper and sugar. Fold in the softly whipped cream; do not over-mix or the sauce will curdle.

This sauce keeps for 2–3 days and may also be served with roast beef; cover so that it doesn't pick up flavours in the fridge.

Fish

At long last in Ireland we're beginning to realise that fish is not a penance. Quite the opposite! Fresh fish, well cooked, is one of the greatest gastronomic pleasures, and we're lucky on this island to have it all around us. Fish is also wonderfully healthy—regarded as 'brain food' by some people, and 'heart food' by others with an interest in keeping cholesterol levels down. Isn't it splendid that something which tastes so good does us good at the same time?

I include in this section Hake in Buttered Crumbs for two reasons. The first is that it is one of those terrific dishes which never fails to please adults and children alike (even fish haters!). The second is that this is a master recipe which can be used for any round fish—cod, haddock, pollock, ling or grey sea mullet. This section also includes the basic technique for making Béchamel Sauce—useful on its own or with many different flavourings (for example, cheese, as in Mornay Sauce), and indispensable for making fish pies. The beauty of Béchamel is that anything coated in it can be reheated perfectly. This is not the case, alas, with grander sauces such as Hollandaise.

I've also given a number of lovely recipes using mussels, the cheapest of all shellfish and the most widely available, both farmed and wild, around Irish coasts. I've noticed that a lot of people love eating mussels in restaurants (huge platefuls of garlicky Mussels Provençale are frequently polished off by individuals who say they can't stand garlic!)—but they are nervous about cooking them at home. Let me reassure any of you who are worried about pollution and possible food poisoning: there really is no cause for concern if you buy from a reliable source, because no fishmonger worth his salt can afford to risk selling unpurified mussels.

As far as freshness is concerned, it's easy to check this yourself. The shells should be tightly shut or should tighten up when tapped against a worktop. The safety rule is simple: if in doubt, throw it out!

Although mussels are available all year round, they are at their best, like oysters, when there is an 'r' in the month. It really is worth learning how to deal with them, because they can be added to so many other fish dishes for variety. And on their own they are divine. What could be nicer for supper than a bowl of freshly cooked mussels served with a good home-made mayonnaise and some crusty brown soda bread!

Both Monkfish Steamed in its Own Juices with Tomato and Dill and Three-minute Fish are favourites of mine, shown to me by that wonderful English cook Jane Grigson who has been such an inspiration. The first is useful because it works equally well with monkfish, halibut, sea bass or turbot. The second is simply the fastest fish dish I know. A mixture of pink and white fish looks especially pretty, and a good fruity olive oil gives a marvellous flavour. Timing is crucial, however. The eaters must be at the table, poised, the minute the oven door is opened!

Béchamel Sauce

$\frac{1}{2}$ pint (300 ml/1$\frac{1}{4}$ cups) milk
a few slices of carrot
a few slices of onion
a small sprig of thyme
a small sprig of parsley

3 peppercorns
1$\frac{1}{2}$ ozs (45 g/scant $\frac{1}{3}$ cup) roux
(see glossary)
salt and freshly ground pepper

This is a marvellous quick way of making Béchamel Sauce if you already have roux made. Put the cold milk into a saucepan with the carrot, onion, peppercorns, thyme and parsley. Bring to the boil, simmer for 4–5 minutes, remove from the heat and leave to infuse for ten minutes. Strain out the vegetables, bring the milk back to the boil and thicken with roux to a light coating consistency. Season with salt and freshly ground pepper, taste and correct the seasoning if necessary.

Ballycotton Fish Pie

Serves 6–8

Many different types of fish may be used for a fish pie, so feel free to adapt this recipe a little to suit your needs. Periwinkles would be a good and cheap addition and a little smoked haddock is tasty also.

$2\frac{1}{2}$ lbs (1.125 kg) fillets of cod, haddock, ling, hake *or* pollock *or* a mixture
18 cooked mussels (optional, see page 29)
1 pint (600 ml/$2\frac{1}{2}$ cups) milk and a very little cream (optional)
4 ozs (110 g/1 cup) onions
3 *or* 4 slices of carrot
1 small bay leaf
a sprig of thyme
3 peppercorns

roux made with 1 oz (30 g) butter and 1 oz (30 g) flour (see glossary)
4 hard-boiled eggs
2 tablesp. ($\frac{1}{4}$ cup) chopped parsley
6 ozs (170 g/$1\frac{3}{4}$ cups) sliced mushrooms
2 lbs (900 g) Duchesse Potato *or* soft mashed potato (see page 63)

Accompaniment
Maître d'Hôtel Butter *or* Garlic Butter (optional)

Put the onions, carrot, bay leaf, thyme and peppercorns into the milk, bring to the boil and simmer for 3–4 minutes. Remove from the heat and leave to infuse for 10–15 minutes. Strain.

Meanwhile, hard-boil the eggs for 10 minutes in boiling water, cool and shell. Sauté the sliced mushrooms in a little butter in a hot pan, season with salt and freshly ground pepper and set aside.

Put the fish into a wide pan or frying pan and cover with the flavoured milk. Season with salt and freshly ground pepper. Cover and simmer gently until the fish is cooked. Take out the fish, carefully removing any bones or skin. Bring the liquid to the boil and thicken with roux; add a little cream (optional) and the chopped parsley, roughly chopped hard-boiled eggs, mushrooms, pieces of fish and the mussels. Stir gently, taste and correct the seasoning. Spoon into 1 large or 6–8 small dishes and pipe Duchesse Potato on top. The pie may be prepared ahead to this point.

Put into a moderate oven 180°C/350°F/regulo 4 to reheat and slightly brown the potato on top, 10–15 minutes approx. if the filling and potato are warm, or 30 minutes approx. if reheating the dish from the cold.

Serve with Garlic Butter or Maître d'Hôtel Butter.

Maître d'Hôtel Butter

2 ozs (55 g/½ stick) butter
4 teasp. finely chopped parsley

juice of ¼ lemon

Cream the butter, then stir in the parsley and a few drops of lemon juice at a time. Roll into butter pats or form into a roll and wrap in greaseproof paper or tin foil, screwing each end so that it looks like a cracker. Refrigerate to harden.

To serve: Remove the tin foil and cut into ¼ inch (5 mm) slices.

Garlic Butter

For Garlic Butter add 2 large crushed cloves of garlic to the above; omit the lemon juice.

Plaice or Sole with Mussels

Serves 6

6 large fillets of black sole or
  plaice, 2¼ lbs (1.1 kg) approx.
½ oz (15 g/⅛ stick) butter
salt and freshly ground pepper
24 mussels

2½ fl ozs (60ml/generous ¼ cup)
  dry white wine
½ oz (15 g/⅛ stick) butter
6 ozs (170 g/2 cups) sliced
  mushrooms

Béchamel Sauce
½ pint (300 ml/1¼ cups) milk
a few slices of carrot
a few slices of onion
a small sprig of thyme
a small sprig of parsley
3 peppercorns
salt and freshly ground pepper

1½ ozs (45 g/scant ⅓ cup) roux (see
  glossary)

Liaison:
1 egg yolk
3 fl ozs (75 ml/scant ½ cup)
  cream

Make the Béchamel Sauce in the usual way (see page 20). Skin the fillets of fish. Smear a little butter over the base of an ovenproof dish.

Tuck in the ends of the fish fillets and arrange in a single layer on the dish. Season with salt and freshly ground pepper. Put the washed mussels into a stainless steel saucepan, add the wine, cover and place on a low heat just until the mussels open, 2–3 minutes. Take the mussels from the shells, remove the beard and keep the mussels aside. Pour the liquid over the fish, cover with tin foil and bake in a moderate oven, 180°C/350°F/regulo 4, until the fish is almost cooked, 10–15 minutes approx.

Meanwhile sauté the mushrooms in a hot pan, season with salt and freshly ground pepper. Strain off the cooking liquor and add it to the Béchamel. Bring it to the boil. Make the liaison by mixing the egg yolks with the cream, add some of the hot liquid to the cold liaison and then mix into the rest of the sauce; taste and correct the seasoning. Sprinkle the mushrooms and mussels over the fish in the serving dish and coat with the sauce (may be made ahead to this point). Return to the oven (160°C/325°F/regulo 3) for 15–20 minutes or until the fish is hot and the sauce is golden on top.

Poached Mackerel with Bretonne Sauce

Serves 6

Fresh mackerel cooked like this is exquisite with Bretonne Sauce; it may be served as a starter or main course.

6 very fresh mackerel	1 teasp. (1 American teasp.) salt
2 pints (1.1 L/5 cups) water	

Bretonne Sauce

2 egg yolks (preferably free-range)	2 tablesp. mixed finely chopped chives, fennel, parsley and thyme
1 teasp. French mustard (we use Maille mustard with green herbs)	6 ozs (170 g/1½ sticks) butter

First make the Bretonne Sauce. Whisk the egg yolks in a bowl with the mustard and finely chopped herbs. Bring the butter to the boil and pour it in a steady stream onto the egg yolks, whisking continuously until the sauce thickens to a light coating consistency like a Hollandaise. Keep warm in a flask, or place in a pottery or plastic bowl (*not* stainless steel), in a saucepan of hot but not boiling water.

Cut the heads off the mackerel, gut and clean but keep whole. Bring water to the boil and add salt and the mackerel. Bring back to boiling point, cover and remove from the heat.

After about 5–8 minutes, check to see whether the fish are cooked. The flesh should lift off the bone. Remove the mackerel onto a plate, scrape off the skin and carefully lift the fillets off the bones and onto a serving plate. Coat carefully with warm sauce. Serve with a good green salad and perhaps some new potatoes.

Hake in Buttered Crumbs*

Serves 6–8

This dish is particularly good served with Buttered Leeks. The recipe for Buttered Leeks is on page 64. This is a master recipe which may be used for almost any round fish, e.g. cod, pollock, ling, haddock and grey sea mullet. My children particularly love fish cooked in this way.

2¼ lbs (1.1 kg) hake

salt and freshly ground pepper
½ oz (15 g/⅛ stick) butter

Mornay Sauce
1 pint (600 ml/2½ cups) milk
a few slices of carrot and onion
3 *or* 4 peppercorns
a sprig of thyme and parsley
2 ozs (55 g/⅓ cup) roux approx.
1 tablesp. chopped parsley
   (optional)

5–6 ozs (140–170 g/1¼–1½ cups)
   grated Cheddar cheese *or* 3 ozs
   (85 g/¾ cup) grated Parmesan
   cheese
¼ teasp. mustard, preferably
   Dijon
salt and freshly ground pepper

Buttered Crumbs
2 ozs (55 g/½ stick) butter

4 ozs (110 g/2 cups) soft, white
   breadcrumbs

1¾ lbs (790 g) Duchesse Potato
   approx. (optional, see page
   63)

First make the Mornay Sauce. Put the cold milk into a saucepan with a few slices of carrot and onion, 3 or 4 peppercorns and a sprig of thyme and parsley. Bring to the boil, simmer for 4–5 minutes, remove from the heat and leave to infuse for 10 minutes if you have enough time. Strain out the vegetables, bring the milk back to the boil and thicken with roux to a light coating consistency. Add the mustard and two-thirds of the grated cheese; keep the remainder of the cheese for sprinkling over the top. Season with salt and freshly ground pepper, taste and correct the seasoning if necessary. Add optional parsley.

Next make the Buttered Crumbs. Melt the butter in a pan and stir in 4 ozs (110 g/2 cups) white breadcrumbs. Remove from the heat immediately and allow to cool.

Skin the fish and cut into portions: 6 ozs (170 g) for a main course, 3 ozs (85 g) for a starter. Season with salt and freshly ground pepper. Lay the pieces of fish in a lightly buttered ovenproof dish, coat with the Mornay Sauce, mix the remaining grated cheese with the Buttered Crumbs and sprinkle over the top. Pipe a ruff of fluffy Duchesse Potato around the edge if you want to have a whole meal in one dish.

Cook in a moderate oven, 180°C/350°F/regulo 4, for 25–30 minutes or until the fish is cooked through and the top is golden brown and crispy. If necessary, place under the grill for a minute or two before you serve, to brown the edges of the potato.

Note: Hake with Buttered Crumbs may be served in individual dishes; scallop shells are particularly attractive, are completely ovenproof and may be used over and over again.

Monkfish Steamed in its Own Juices with Tomato and Dill*

Serves 4

This is a superb recipe originally shown to me by Jane Grigson. She used halibut, but we have found that it may be adapted to many kinds of fish, e.g. sea bass, grey sea mullet, turbot or brill.

$1\frac{1}{2}$ lbs (675 g) monkfish tail
1 oz (30 g/$\frac{1}{4}$ stick) butter
salt, freshly ground pepper and sugar
1 tablesp. finely chopped dill
1 tablesp. finely chopped parsley

1 small, very finely chopped shallot
2 very ripe tomatoes, peeled, seeded and flesh cut into $\frac{1}{4}$ inch (5 mm) dice (concassé)

1 x 14 inches (35.5 cm) sauté pan
 or frying pan with a lid

Trim the monkfish tail of all skin and membrane. Cut the flesh into $\frac{1}{4}$ inch (5 mm) collops.

25

Prepare the tomato concassé (see glossary), and season with salt, freshly ground pepper and sugar.

Chop the parsley and dill and finely dice the shallot. Grease the base of the sauté pan with half of the butter, scatter with the finely chopped shallot, then arrange the pieces of fish in a single layer. Sprinkle with tomato concassé, chopped parsley and dill. Season with salt and freshly ground pepper. Cut a circle of greaseproof paper to fit inside the pan exactly; smear it with the rest of the butter and place butter side down on top of the fish. Cover with a tight-fitting saucepan lid. Cook on a medium heat for 8 minutes approx. Test, taste, correct the seasoning if necessary and serve right away on 4 hot plates; no garnish is needed.

Serve with a good green salad and perhaps some new potatoes.

Salted Fish with Olive Oil and Herbs

Serves 4

Anne Willan of La Varenne Cookery School in Paris told me about salting fish in this Japanese way; it intensifies the flavour and makes it taste even more delicious.

4 whole fish weighing 1 lb (450 g) each approx. *or* 4 x 6 ozs (170 g) fillets of white fish, e.g. bass, bream, grey sea mullet *or* mackerel
1½ ozs (45 g) coarse sea salt (we use Maldon)

4 fl ozs (100 ml/½ cup) olive oil
2 tablesp. mixed freshly chopped chives, basil and parsley *or* chives, fennel, lemon balm and parsley

If you are using whole fish, gut them carefully, scale if necessary and wash and dry well with kitchen paper. Cut 3 or 4 deep slashes diagonally on each side, almost to the bone. Put the fish on a tray and sprinkle it on both sides with coarse sea salt. Leave in the fridge for 2–3 hours, turning occasionally.

If you are using fish fillets there is no need to slash them, but salt them and leave for 30 minutes approx. When the fish is ready, wash off the salt, dry well, brush lightly with oil and cook on a heavy grill pan until brown on each side and cooked through.

Mix the olive oil with chopped herbs and spoon over the hot fish. Serve immediately on hot plates with a good green salad and perhaps some new potatoes.

Three-minute Fish*

Serves 4

This is the fastest fish recipe I know and certainly one of the most delicious. It can be fun to mix pink- and white-fleshed fish on the same plate, e.g. salmon and sea bass.

1 lb (450 g) very fresh fish, e.g. wild Irish salmon, cod, turbot, large sole, sea bass *or* grey sea mullet olive oil	finely chopped parsley, thyme, chives finely grated rind of 1 small lemon salt and freshly ground pepper

4 ovenproof main course plates

Season the fillet of fish with salt and freshly ground pepper half an hour approx. before cutting; chill in the fridge to stiffen it.

Preheat the oven to 230°C/450°F/regulo 8.

While the oven is heating, brush the plates with olive oil. Put the fillet of fish on a chopping board skin-side down; cut the flesh into scant $\frac{1}{4}$ inch (5 mm) thin slices down onto the skin. Arrange the slices on the base of the plate but don't allow them to overlap or they will cook unevenly. Brush the fish slices with more olive oil, season with salt and freshly ground pepper and sprinkle each plate with a little freshly chopped herbs and lemon zest. Put the plates in the *fully preheated oven* and cook for 3 minutes; you might like to check after 2 minutes if the slices are exceptionally thin. The fish is cooked when it looks opaque.

Rush it to the table, served with crusty white bread, a good green salad and a glass of dry white wine.

Smoked Haddock with Parmesan

Serves 6

Smoked Haddock is available all around the country. Try to find smoked Finnan haddock which has not been dyed as well as smoked.

1½ lbs (675 g) smoked Finnan
  haddock
1 pint (600 ml/2½ cups) milk
a few slices of carrot
a few slices of onion
bouquet garni
2 ozs (55 g/⅓ cup) roux (see
  glossary)

2 tablesp. (¼ cup) chopped
  parsley
4 ozs (110 g/1¼ cups) grated
  cheese (preferably Parmesan
  but mature Cheddar would be
  wonderful too)
Buttered Crumbs (see page 24)
1¾ lbs (470 g) Duchesse Potato
  approx. (see page 63)

Put the cold milk into a saucepan with the carrot, onion and bouquet garni. Bring slowly to the boil and simmer for 3–4 minutes; remove from the heat and leave to infuse for 10–15 minutes. Strain. Meanwhile cover the smoked haddock with cold water, bring slowly to the boil, then discard the water. Cover the haddock with the flavoured milk and simmer for 10 minutes approx. or until just cooked. Remove the haddock to the serving dish with a perforated spoon.

Bring the milk back to the boil, thicken with roux to a light coating consistency, add the parsley and half the cheese, taste and pour over the haddock in the dish. Sprinkle with a mixture of buttered crumbs and the remainder of the grated cheese. Pipe Duchesse Potato around the outside of the dish (may be prepared ahead to this point). Reheat in a moderate oven, 180°C/350°F/regulo 4, for 15–20 minutes or until the top is crispy and bubbly and the potato edges are golden.

Cod with Dijon Mustard Sauce

Serves 6

2 ozs (55 g/½ stick) butter
8 ozs (225 g/2 cups) chopped
  onions
2 lbs (900 g) fresh cod fillets
1 pint (600 ml/2½ cups) milk
2 fl ozs (50 ml/¼ cup) cream
2–3 tablesp. Dijon or English
  mustard

1 oz (50 g/scant ¼ cup) flour
1 tablesp. chopped parsley
salt and freshly ground pepper
1¾ lbs (790 g) Duchesse Potato
  (optional, see page 63)

Melt the butter and sweat the onions in a covered saucepan until golden brown. Skin the cod and cut into portions. Season with salt and freshly ground pepper. Put into a wide saucepan or frying pan, cover with milk and cream, bring to the boil and simmer gently for 4–6 minutes, depending on the thickness of the fish. Remove the fish carefully to a serving dish. Add 1 oz (30 g) flour to the onions, stir and cook for 2 minutes. Add in the hot milk and bring back to the boil, then simmer for 3–4 minutes. Add the mustard and chopped parsley; taste and correct the seasoning, then pour over the fish and serve.

Duchesse Potato may be piped around this dish. It may be allowed to cool and reheated later in a moderate oven, 180°C/350°F/regulo 4, for 20 minutes approx.

Moules Provençale*

Serves 6–8

Mussels are a perennial favourite; don't skimp on the garlic in this recipe or they will taste rather dull and 'bready'.

48 mussels, approx. 3½–4 lbs (1.575–1.8 kg)

Provençale Butter
3 ozs (85 g/¾ stick) soft butter
2 large cloves of garlic
2 tablesp. (¼ cup) finely chopped parsley

1 tablesp. (4 American teasp.) olive oil
fresh, white breadcrumbs

Check that all the mussels are closed. If any are open, tap the mussel on the work top; if it does not close within a few seconds, discard. (The rule with shellfish is always, 'If in doubt, throw it out'.) Scrape off any barnacles from the mussel shells. Wash the mussels well in several changes of cold water. Then spread them in a single layer in a pan, cover with a folded tea-towel or a lid and cook over a gentle heat. This usually takes 2–3 minutes; the mussels are cooked just as soon as the shells open. Remove them from the pan immediately or they will shrink in size and become tough.

Remove the beard (the little tuft of tough 'hair' which attached the mussel to the rock or rope it grew on). Discard one shell. Loosen the mussel from the other shell, but leave it in the shell. Allow to get quite cold.

Meanwhile make the Provençale Butter. Peel and crush the garlic and pound it in a mortar with the finely chopped parsley and olive oil. Gradually beat in the butter (this may be done either in a bowl or a food processor). Spread the garlic butter over the mussels in the shells and dip each one into the soft, white breadcrumbs. They may be prepared ahead to this point and frozen in a covered box lined with cling-film or tin foil.

Arrange in individual serving dishes. Brown under the grill and serve with crusty white bread to mop up the delicious garlicky juices.

Cockles or Palourdes Provençale

For those of you unfamiliar with the word Palourdes, it is a type of clam which grows off the West Cork coast, around Kenmare Bay.

48 cockles *or* **Palourdes**   **fresh, white breadcrumbs**
Provençale Butter (see above)

Prepare in the same way as Moules Provençale.

Poultry

The starting point here is not first catch your chicken, as Mrs Beeton might have said, but first find yourself a good *free-range* chicken. As I've said before, the flavour is infinitely superior to intensively reared chickens. Fortunately, as more and more people discover the difference for themselves, free-range poultry is becoming more widely available. There are degrees of free-range, however, so do ask questions and keep looking until you find a good source.

The other thing you might like to seek out is an 'old hen', cheaper and even better suited to the Chicken Pilaff recipe than a chicken. Hens are undeservedly scorned nowadays. They have actually been rechristened 'casserole roasters' by the poultry trade to give them a new air of respectability! This is one recipe that proves how tasty they can be. It also proves that it is possible to feed a large crowd of people easily and economically. My mother-in-law, Myrtle Allen, used to cook this Chicken Pilaff recipe when her children were hungry teenagers, given to inviting other hungry teenagers home for impromptu parties.

Poached Turkey with Mushrooms shows how successfully turkey can be treated in a similar way, with mushrooms added to the sauce for extra excitement—but the turkey should be free-range too, because that special flavour comes through in the poaching.

Equally comforting is Farmhouse Chicken, a recipe from my childhood. A big black roasting tin of this, taken from the Aga, would feed our whole family—once we had stopped fighting over the crispy potatoes on top! It could of course be put in something more glamorous than a roasting tin, although that's the way it still tastes best to me.

For the days when you simply haven't time for any of these recipes, Chicken Breasts with Cream and Lemon Juice is the answer. You can rush into the shops on your way home to buy the chicken breasts and have them on the table, tasting delectable, in fifteen minutes—just long enough to rustle up Tomato Fondue (see page 67) or a simple green salad to set them off.

Chicken Pilaff*

Serves 8

This delicious chicken recipe can be a very economical way to serve large numbers for a party. Serve with a Pilaff Rice (see below) and Tomato Fondue (see page 67) and garnish with sprigs of parsley or watercress. It may be prepared ahead of time and reheats well but do not add the liaison until just before serving.

1 x 4–4½ lbs (1.8–2 kg) approx. boiling fowl *or* good free-range chicken
1 large sliced carrot
1 large sliced onion
5 peppercorns
a bouquet garni made up of a sprig of thyme, parsley stalks, a tiny bay leaf, a stick of celery

¾ pint(450 ml/scant 2 cups) approx. water *or* water and white wine mixed *or* light chicken stock (*Simply Delicious*, page 35)
1 oz (30g) approx. roux (see glossary)
6 fl ozs (175 ml/¾ cup) cream
salt and freshly ground pepper

Liaison
1 egg yolk

2 fl ozs (50 ml/¼ cup) cream

Pilaff Rice
1 oz (30 g/¼ stick) butter
2 tablesp. finely chopped onion *or* shallot
14 ozs (400 g/2 cups) long-grain rice (preferably Basmati)

32 fl ozs (975 ml/4 cups) home-made chicken stock (*Simply Delicious*, page 35)
salt and freshly ground pepper

Season the chicken with salt and freshly ground pepper; put into a heavy casserole with the carrot, celery, onion, herbs and peppercorns. Pour in water, water and wine or stock. Cover and bring to the boil and simmer either on top of the stove or in the oven for 1½–3 hours, depending on the age of the bird. When the bird is cooked, remove from the casserole.

Strain and de-grease the cooking liquid and return to the casserole. Discard the vegetables: they have already given their flavour to the cooking liquid. Reduce the liquid in an uncovered casserole for a few minutes. If it tastes a little weak, add cream and reduce again; thicken to a light coating consistency with roux (see glossary). Taste, add salt, correct the seasoning. Skin the chicken and carve the flesh into 2-inch (5 cm) pieces; add the meat to the sauce and allow it to heat through and bubble (the dish may be prepared ahead to this point).

Hake in Buttered Crumbs

Buttered Prawns with Bretonne Sauce

Chicken Pilaff and Tomato Fondue

Glazed Loin of Bacon

Ballymaloe Bacon Chop

Finally, just before serving mix the egg yolk and cream to make a liaison. Add some of the hot sauce to the liaison then carefully stir into the chicken mixture. Taste, correct the seasoning and stir well but do not allow to boil further or the sauce will curdle.

Pilaff Rice: Melt the butter in a casserole, add the finely chopped onion and sweat for 2–3 minutes. Add the rice and toss for a minute or two until the grains change colour. Season with salt and freshly ground pepper, add the chicken stock, cover and bring to the boil. Simmer either on top of the stove or in the oven for 10 minutes approx., or until the rice is just cooked and all the water is absorbed.

Note: Basmati rice cooks quite quickly; other types of rice may take up to 15 minutes.

Poached Turkey with Mushrooms

Serves 20–25 approx.

A great dish for a party, it may be made up ahead and reheated.

1 x 10 lbs (4.5 kg) turkey (preferably free-range)
2 large carrots
2 large onions
2 sticks of celery
a bouquet garni made up of 6 parsley stalks, 2 sprigs of thyme, 1 small bay leaf, 1 sprig of tarragon
10 peppercorns

6 pints (3.4 L/15 cups) light chicken stock (*Simply Delicious*, page 35) *or* water
salt and freshly ground pepper
2 lbs (900 g) mushrooms
1–2 ozs (30–55 g) butter
1½ pints (900 ml/3¾ cups) cream *or* cream and milk
4 ozs (110 g) roux approx.

Garnish
flat parsley

Put the turkey into a large saucepan. Pour in the chicken stock or water, add 2 large sliced carrots, 2 onions cut into quarters, 2 sticks of celery, the bouquet garni and some peppercorns. Season with salt and freshly ground pepper. Bring to the boil, cover and simmer on top of the stove or in a moderate oven, 180°C/350°F/regulo 4, for 2–2½ hours. When the turkey is cooked, remove from the pot, strain and de-grease the cooking liquid. Discard the vegetables—they will have given their flavour to the cooking juices already. Reduce the liquid by one-half.

Meanwhile sauté the sliced mushrooms in a little butter on a very hot pan and keep aside. Add 1½ pints (900 ml/3¾ cups) cream or creamy milk to the turkey poaching liquid, reduce again for 5–10 minutes, thicken with 4 ozs (110 g) roux approx., to a light coating consistency. Add the mushrooms and taste. Skin the turkey, carve the flesh into 2 inch (5 cm) pieces approx. and add to the sauce. Bring back to the boil, taste and correct the seasoning if necessary. Put into a hot serving dish and garnish with flat parsley.

Alternatively, put it into several large serving dishes, pipe a ruff of Duchesse Potato around the edges (see page 63) and reheat later in a moderate oven, 180°C/350°F/regulo 4, for 20–30 minutes.

Serve with a good green salad. Pilaff Rice would be delicious also instead of potato (see page 32).

Farmhouse Chicken

Serves 8

A whole meal in a dish, this was a favourite family supper in our house. We used to serve it in a big, black roasting tin.

1 x 3½ lbs (1.575 kg) free-range chicken	12 ozs (340 g approx.) thinly sliced carrots
seasoned flour	5 lbs (2.3 kg) large 'old' potatoes approx.
1¼ lbs (560 g) streaky bacon in one piece	salt and freshly ground pepper
2 tablesp. (⅛ cup) sunflower *or* arachide oil	2 pints (1.1 L) chicken stock, made from the giblets and carcass (*Simply Delicious*, page 35)
14 ozs (400 g approx.) finely sliced *or* chopped onions	

Garnish
1 tablesp. freshly chopped
  parsley

deep roasting tin 15″ (38 cm) square approx.

Preheat the oven to 230°C/450°F/regulo 8.

Joint the chicken into 8 pieces; separate the wing joints so they will cook evenly. Cut the rind off the bacon; cut 8 ozs (225 g) into ½ inch (1 cm) lardons and the remainder into ¼ inch (5 mm) thick slices. If salty, blanch, refresh and dry on kitchen paper. Heat the oil in a wide frying pan and cook the lardons until the fat begins to run and they are pale golden; transfer to a plate. Toss the chicken joints in seasoned flour, sauté in the bacon fat and oil until golden on both sides, remove from the pan and put with the bacon. Finally toss the onions and carrots in bacon fat for 1–2 minutes.

Peel the potatoes and slice a little less than half into $\frac{1}{4}$ inch (5 mm) rounds. Arrange a layer of potato slices on the bottom of the deep roasting tin. Season with salt and freshly ground pepper. Sprinkle the carrots, onions and bacon over the potatoes and arrange the chicken on top. Season again with salt and freshly ground pepper. Cut the remaining potatoes into thick slices lengthways, $1\frac{1}{2}$ inches (4 cm) approx., and arrange cut side up on top of the chicken (the whole top of the dish should be covered with potato slices). Season with salt and freshly ground pepper. Pour in the chicken stock.

Bake in the preheated oven for 1 hour approx. After 30 minutes put the strips of bacon on top so they get deliciously crisp with the potatoes. Test after 1 hour — it may take a little longer. Cover loosely with greaseproof paper or foil near the end of cooking; if it is getting too brown, sprinkle with chopped parsley and serve.

Chicken Breasts with Cream and Lemon Juice

Serves 4

4 chicken breasts	$\frac{1}{4}$ pint (150 ml/scant $\frac{3}{4}$ cup) chicken
1 lemon	stock (*Simply Delicious*, **page 35**)
$\frac{1}{2}$ oz (15 g/$\frac{1}{8}$ stick) butter	salt and freshly ground pepper
$\frac{1}{4}$ pint (150 ml/scant $\frac{3}{4}$ cup) cream	1–2 tablesp. chopped parsley

Grate the rind from the lemon on the finest part of the grater; keep aside. Squeeze the juice from half of the lemon, dip the chicken breasts in it and keep the rest for later. Season with salt and freshly ground pepper. Melt a little butter in a sauté pan which is wide enough to take the breasts in a single layer. Toss the breasts in butter, cover with a butter wrapper and lid and cook gently on top or in a moderate oven, 180°C/350°F/regulo 4, for 10 minutes approx. (depending on the size of the breasts). Be careful not to overcook them or they will be dry.

Remove the breasts to a warm dish, de-glaze the pan with the stock and stir to dissolve any little crusty bits remaining. Add the cream and reduce, taste and season if necessary. Add a little lemon rind, a squeeze of lemon juice and the chopped parsley, then taste again. Spoon the sauce over the chicken breasts and serve immediately with Tomato Fondue (see page 67) and a good green salad.

Pork and Bacon

I absolutely love Irish bacon; it has a unique flavour quite unlike bacon from any other country, yet somehow it is looked on as the 'poor relation' of other meats and considered by many to be 'fine' for a family meal, but nothing like 'grand' enough for entertaining—I don't agree, I quite often serve Glazed Loin of Bacon for a dinner party with Piperonata or Tomato Fondue and either Colcannon or Champ and every scrap disappears! It never fails to re-convert people to the most traditional of Irish meats. However, a word of caution: if you want to find really good bacon you have to search carefully. I buy my bacon from several sources, one being a pork and bacon shop in Cork which has been in the same family for three generations. They choose their bacon carefully and exact a high standard from their suppliers so that the bacon and pork is not tainted with strong flavours or cured with too much salt. The result is delicious sweet bacon that leaves one licking one's lips and wishing for more.

Bacon is also extremely versatile. The Glazed Loin of Bacon recipe can be used not only for a loin, but also for a ham or oyster cut (that lovely piece between the loin and the ham). The ham looks very splendid in all its glory and will feed fifteen to twenty people, but can be tricky to carve. The advantage of the loin is that carving it is so easy and the piece of meat can be as large as you like.

Ballymaloe Bacon Chop is unbelievably easy and surprisingly delicious served with Fried Banana and even better with an accompaniment of Irish Whiskey Sauce. Ham Morvandelle, on the other hand, is a special party piece, perfect for a large number of people. It requires the best part of a bottle of Chablis (any old wine will, alas, *not* do for cooking!), but the flavour is quite superb.

The pork dishes are equally varied, starting with another favourite, Roast Pork with Garlic and Thyme Leaves and (the classic accompaniment) good Apple Sauce. We quite often use streaky pork in this, but one could, of course, use loin instead. I've included Roast Kassler, too, because I think this type of pork, which has been marinated with juniper berries and spices and then smoked, is one of the most delicious new products to come on the Irish market in the last few years.

For something entirely different, I hope you will try Filipino Pork with Peppers and Fresh Ginger—a simple and not too spicy oriental recipe which one of my assistants tested in the cookery school at lunchtime recently and was duly rewarded with empty plates.

Glazed Loin of Bacon*

Serves 12–15

This recipe turns bacon into a feast—grand enough for any dinner party. It is particularly good served with Tomato Fondue, Piperonata, Colcannon or Ulster Champ.

4–5 lbs (1.8–2.25 kg) best-quality loin of bacon, either smoked or unsmoked, off the bone	$\frac{3}{4}$ lb (340 g/1$\frac{3}{4}$ cups) brown Demerara sugar
1 small tin (14 ozs/400 g) of pineapple	20–30 whole cloves approx.

Cover the bacon in cold water and bring slowly to the boil. If the bacon is very salty there will be a white froth on top of the water; in this case it is preferable to discard the water. It may be necessary to change the water several times depending on how salty the bacon is. Finally, cover the bacon with hot water and then simmer until almost cooked. Allow 15 minutes approx. to the pound. Remove the rind, cut the fat into a diamond pattern and stud with cloves. Blend brown sugar to a thick paste with a little pineapple juice, 3–4 tablesp. approx. Be careful not to make it too liquid. Spread this over the bacon. Bake in a fully preheated hot oven, 250°C/475°F/regulo 9, for 20–30 minutes or until the top has caramelised. While it is glazing, baste with juices every few minutes.

This is delicious on a cold buffet when cooked the same day. Cold buffet food is best freshly cooked and not too cold. Glazed Loin of Bacon may be served hot or cold.

The recipes for Piperonata, Colcannon and Buttered Cabbage are on pages 61, 62 and 67 respectively.

Ballymaloe Bacon Chop*

Serves 4–5 approx.

In the restaurant at Ballymaloe we serve Bacon Chop with Irish Whiskey Sauce, but it is also delicious served just with Fried Banana.

2 lbs (900 g) loin of bacon (boneless and without the streaky end)	1 egg and some milk fresh, white breadcrumbs
4 ozs (110 g/scant 1 cup) seasoned flour	

For frying
1 oz (30 g/$\frac{1}{4}$ stick) Clarified Butter
   (see page 16) *or* $\frac{1}{2}$ oz (15 g/
   $\frac{1}{8}$ stick) butter and 1–2 tablesp.
   olive oil

Use freshly cured green bacon. Cover the piece of bacon with cold water. Bring to the boil. If the bacon is salty, throw out the water and start again; you may need to do this twice or in extreme cases three times. Boil for 30 minutes approx. or until it is three-quarters cooked. Remove the rind and trim away any surplus fat. Slice into chops $\frac{1}{2}$–$\frac{3}{4}$ inches (1–2 cm) thick. Dip in seasoned flour, then in beaten egg and finally coat with white breadcrumbs. Heat Clarified Butter and oil in a heavy frying pan; fry the chops gently until they are cooked through and golden on both sides.

For a special treat, serve with Irish Whiskey Sauce.

Note: For a cheaper version, streaky bacon could be used instead of loin.

Fried Banana

2 bananas $\frac{1}{2}$ oz (15 g/$\frac{1}{8}$ stick) butter

Melt the butter in a frying pan; peel the bananas. Split the bananas in half lengthways or cut in thick slices diagonally. Fry gently in the melted butter until soft and slightly golden. Serve hot with Ballymaloe Bacon Chop.

Irish Whiskey Sauce

8 ozs (225 g/1 cup) castor sugar   6 tablesp. (generous $\frac{1}{3}$ cup) Irish
3 fl ozs (80 ml/$\frac{1}{3}$ cup) cold water   whiskey
                                       2$\frac{1}{2}$ fl ozs (60 ml) hot water

Put the castor sugar into a bowl with water; stir over a gentle heat until the sugar dissolves and syrup comes to the boil. Remove the spoon and do not stir. Continue to boil until it turns a nice chestnut-brown colour. Remove from the heat and immediately add 2$\frac{1}{2}$ fl ozs (60 ml) of hot water. Allow to dissolve again and then add 6 tablespoons ($\frac{1}{2}$ cup) of Irish whiskey. Serve hot or cold.

Ham Morvandelle

Serves 16–20

This is another recipe suitable for a party, but rather more extravagant than Chicken Pilaff. It freezes well and reheats perfectly. The recipe comes from the Burgundy area of France and takes its name from the Morvan forests.

1 x 8–10 lbs (3.4–4.5 kg) ham
1 oz (30 g/¼ stick) butter
1 tablesp. oil
½ lb (225 g) sliced carrots
½ lb (225 g) sliced onions
12 parsley sprigs
1 bay leaf
12 peppercorns

a sprig of thyme
4 cloves
½ bottle of white Burgundy, e.g. Chablis *or* Pouilly Fuissé (we use a Petit Chablis)
1¼ pints (900 ml) home-made chicken stock (*Simply Delicious*, page 35)

Sauce
2 lbs (900 g) sliced mushrooms
4 tablesp. chopped onion *or* shallot

salt and freshly ground pepper
18 fl ozs (475 ml) cream

Roux
4 ozs (110 g/1 stick) butter

4 ozs (110 g) flour

Liaison
3 egg yolks

2 fl ozs (50 ml) cream

Soak the ham in cold water overnight and discard the water the next day. Place the ham in a large saucepan and cover with fresh, cold water. Bring it slowly to the boil and discard the water. Repeat the process once or twice more, depending on how salty the ham is. (This is particularly important if the dish is to be frozen because freezing seems to intensify the salty taste.)

Meanwhile, melt the butter and oil in a casserole large enough to take the ham. Toss the sliced carrots and onions in the fat and sweat for 10 minutes approx. Place the ham on top of the vegetables and add the parsley, bay leaf, peppercorns, thyme and cloves. Pour over the wine and stock; cover, bring to the boil and simmer on top of the stove or in a moderate oven, 180°C/350°F/regulo 4, until the ham is cooked, 2½–3 hours approx. You can test when it is cooked by lifting the skin: if it peels off easily, the ham is cooked. (Allow 15 minutes approx. to the lb (450 g) and 15 minutes over.)

40

To make the sauce cook the onion or shallot in a little butter on a low heat until soft. Remove from the pan. Sauté the mushrooms on a high heat and add to the shallot. When the ham is cooked, strain and de-grease the cooking liquid. Return the liquid to the casserole with 18 fl ozs (475 ml) cream and bring to the boil. Thicken with roux to a light coating consistency and simmer for 5 minutes. Add the mushrooms and shallots and taste for seasoning. Skin the ham and slice carefully, arrange in one or more serving dishes.

To make the liaison, mix the egg yolks with 2 fl ozs (50 ml) cream and add a ladleful of the simmering sauce to the liaison, mix well and add into the remaining sauce. Do not allow to boil again or it may curdle.

Spoon the sauce over the slices of ham in the serving dish (may be prepared ahead to this point). Reheat in a moderate oven, 180°C/350°F/regulo 4, for 20–30 minutes approx. It should be bubbling and slightly golden on top.

For a dinner party, you may want to pipe a border of Duchesse Potatoes (see page 63) around the outside of the serving dish. Tomato Fondue (see page 67), Piperonata (see page 61) and a good Green Salad (see page 60) make nice accompaniments.

Note: Loin or oyster cut of bacon may be used for this recipe.

Roast Kassler

Serves 10–12

That delicious German speciality, Kassler, is actually fresh loin of pork marinated with pepper, cloves and juniper berries for 12–24 hours and then oak-smoked for a further 12 hours. It used to be quite difficult to find but is now becoming more widely available as many pork butchers produce their own. It is best roasted rather than boiled. It may be served hot, warm or cold.

1 x 5 lbs (2.25 kg) Kassler

Preheat the oven to 180°C/350°F/regulo 4.

Weigh the joint and calculate 20 minutes per 1 lb (450 g). Put the piece of Kassler onto a roasting tin; during cooking, baste once or twice with the fat which will render out. Test the meat. The juices should run clear. When cooked, turn off the oven or set to a very low heat; leave the meat to relax for 20 minutes approx. before carving. De-grease the pan and serve the sweet juices with the Kassler. Keep the pork fat to roast or sauté potatoes.

Roast Pork with Garlic and Thyme Leaves and Apple Sauce

Serves 10–12

Streaky pork makes the sweetest and juiciest roast of pork; make sure to buy it with the skin on to get the crackling.

1 x 5 lbs (2.3 kg) joint of streaky pork

Mix or liquidise the following:

3 cloves of finely chopped garlic
4 tablesp. parsley
1 tablesp. olive oil (add more if needed to make a thick paste)

2 tablesp. fresh thyme leaves
1 teasp. salt
1 teasp. freshly ground black pepper

Gravy
1 pint (600 ml/2½ cups) home-made chicken stock (*Simply Delicious*, page 35)
roux (optional)

Score the skin at ¼ inch (5 mm) intervals—let your butcher do this if possible because the skin is quite tough. (This will also make it easier to carve later.) Rub in the herb paste.

Preheat the oven to 190°C/375°F/regulo 5. Roast on a rack, allowing 25–28 minutes per lb (450 g).

Note: Just before the end of cooking turn up temperature to very hot, 230°C/450°F/regulo 8, to get crisp crackling.

To make gravy, de-grease the roasting pan and add 1 pint (600 ml/2½ cups) chicken stock to de-glaze the pan. Bring to the boil. Season and thicken with a little roux if desired (see glossary). Freshly chopped herbs may be added to the gravy. Serve with crispy, roast potatoes and Apple Sauce.

Apple Sauce

Serves 10 approx.

The trick with Apple Sauce is to cook it covered on a low heat with very little water.

1 lb (450 g) cooking apples, e.g.
    Bramley Seedling *or* Grenadier
1–2 dessertsp. water
	2 ozs (55 g/⅓ cup) sugar,
	    depending on how tart the
	    apples are

Peel, quarter and core the apples. Cut the pieces into two and put in a stainless steel or cast-iron saucepan with sugar and water. Cover and put over a low heat. As soon as the apple has broken down, beat into a purée, stir and taste for sweetness. Serve warm.

Note: Apple Sauce freezes perfectly, so make more than you need and freeze in tiny, plastic cartons. It is also a good way to use up windfalls.

Filipino Pork with Peppers and Fresh Ginger

Serves 6 approx.

Oriental meat recipes make the most of a little meat. This delicious pork dish was cooked for me by Susie Noriega.

1 lb (450 g) pork fillet	1½ ozs (45 g) bamboo shoots
2 tablesp. (⅛ cup) light soya sauce	1½ ozs (45 g) unsalted peanuts
2 small green peppers	1 teasp. tapioca
a large clove of garlic	2½ fl ozs (60 ml/generous ¼ cup)
4 large spring onions	water approx.
1 x 1″ (2.5 cm) fresh ginger root	1 tablesp. tabasco *or* oyster sauce
1 fresh red *or* green chilli	a pinch of sugar
2 tablesp. (⅛ cup) arachide oil	freshly ground pepper

1 wok

Cut the pork into ¼ inch (5 mm) strips, marinate in light soya sauce, season with freshly ground pepper and leave aside. Put the peanuts on a baking sheet and roast for 20 minutes approx. in a moderate oven, 180°C/350°F/regulo 4, until golden. Rub off the loose skins.

Halve the chilli and remove the seeds. Cut into small dice. Cut the bamboo shoots in pieces the same size as the pork. Halve and quarter the green pepper, remove the seeds and cut into similar-sized pieces.

Peel the ginger root and garlic and chop finely. Also chop the spring onions finely on the bias.

Heat the wok, add 1 tablespoon of arachide oil and fry the garlic, ginger and spring onions for a few seconds. Remove to a plate. Heat the wok to very hot, add the other tablespoon of oil, toss the pork for 2 minutes maximum and then add in the rest of the vegetables. Season with salt and freshly ground pepper, add a drop of water, cover and cook for 3–4 minutes until the vegetables are cooked but still crunchy. Then add the chilli and roasted peanuts. Dissolve 1 teaspoon of tapioca in $2\frac{1}{2}$ fl ozs (60 ml/generous $\frac{1}{4}$ cup) of water approx., add a dash of tabasco or oyster sauce and a pinch of sugar. Add to the wok, bubble up again and serve immediately in a hot serving dish with plain boiled rice.

Lamb and Beef

Both Myrtle Allen and I are interested in collecting traditional Irish recipes which we believe should be saved from oblivion while there is still time. Sometimes they can be difficult to find: people may have cooked from instinct, putting in a fist of this and a pinch of that, or they may have begun to lose confidence, feeling that in some strange way their old-fashioned, home-cooked food was inferior to newer foods bought in tins or packets. I urge you to record your grandmother's and great-grandmother's recipes before they get lost, no matter how simple they appear.

The Dingle Pie recipe I demonstrate in this series is Myrtle Allen's adaptation of a traditional mutton pie recipe which was made on the Dingle Peninsula. We are convinced that it is a variation of the Cornish Pasty introduced to the south-west of Ireland by Cornish miners who came over in the early nineteenth century to help the locals to mine copper. Myrtle added cumin to the filling — with magical results. The hot water crust pastry which absolutely anyone can master was originally made with mutton fat, but Myrtle substituted butter which results in a light crisp pastry with a delicious flavour. This pastry can of course be used for other pies and it is a great stand-by for people who feel that they absolutely cannot make pastry. The Dingle Pie can be made in advance, eaten hot or cold and frozen cooked or uncooked.

Just as Irish lamb is usually excellent, good Irish beef has no rivals — but it must be said that there is still a great deal of poor-quality beef on sale. Beef is so expensive that I think we need to get the best for our money. It should not only be tender but also taste 'beefy'. Next time beef is on your plate, close your eyes and ask yourself honestly if you can tell by the taste which type of meat you are eating. If you can't, it's time to seek out a better butcher!

The two beef stews I've chosen are full of flavour. The stout gives a wonderful richness to the sauce in the recipe for Beef with Murphy, and few people can identify the secret ingredient, dried orange peel, which imparts a special something with no discernible orange taste at all. Italian Beef Stew is another warming winter dish, a great favourite of my children and their friends. Add the mushrooms at the end of cooking; if you add them at the beginning they will taste and look like bitter little black rags by the end! The great thing about stews like these is that they can, indeed *should*, be prepared in advance, because they actually taste better the next day.

Pan-grilled Steak with Béarnaise Sauce and Pommes Allumettes uses a classic warm French emulsion sauce. Béarnaise Sauce is really worth mastering; and if you can make Hollandaise from *Simply Delicious*, you'll manage this easily. Besides being delicious with steak it is very good indeed with plain roast beef, or even fish or poached eggs. The crispy little Pommes Allumettes are a perfect accompaniment to the steak. I cook them in olive oil to make them taste, yes, simply delicious!

Dingle Pie*

Serves 6

This is a favourite recipe which was adapted by my mother-in-law, Myrtle Allen, from an old traditional recipe. It is wonderful served either hot or cold and makes marvellous picnic food. The secret is the cumin seed, a widely available spice which is particularly good with lamb.

1 lb (450 g) boneless lamb *or* mutton (from the shoulder *or* leg; keep bones for stock)
9 ozs (255 g/2¼ cups) chopped onions
9 ozs (255 g/1¾ cups) chopped carrots

1 good teasp. cumin seed
10 fl ozs (300 ml/1¼ cups) mutton *or* lamb stock
2 tablesp. flour
salt and freshly ground pepper

Stock
lamb bones from the meat
1 carrot
1 onion
outside stalk of celery

a bouquet garni made up of a sprig of thyme, parsley stalks, a small bay leaf

Pastry
1 lb (450 g/3½ cups) flour
9 ozs (275 g/2¼ sticks) butter

6 fl ozs (175 ml/¾ cup) water
a pinch of salt

Egg wash
1 egg

a pinch of salt

2 tins 6 inches (15 cm) in diameter, 1½ inches (4 cm) high

If no stock is available, put the bones, carrots, onions, celery and bouquet garni into a saucepan. Cover with cold water and simmer for 3–4 hours to make a stock. Cut all the surplus fat away from the meat and then cut the meat into small, neat pieces about the size of a small sugar lump. Render down the scraps of fat in a hot, wide saucepan until the fat runs. Discard the pieces. Cut the vegetables into slightly smaller dice and toss them in the fat, leaving them to cook for 3–4 minutes. Remove the vegetables and toss the meat in the remaining fat over a high heat until the colour turns.

Heat the cumin seed in the oven for a few minutes and crush lightly. Stir the flour and cumin seed into the meat. Cook gently for 2 minutes and blend in the stock gradually. Bring to the boil, stirring occasionally. Add back the vegetables, season with salt and freshly ground pepper and leave to simmer in a covered pot. If using young lamb, 30 minutes will be sufficient; an older animal may take up to 1 hour.

Meanwhile, make the pastry. Sieve the flour and salt into a mixing bowl and make a well in the centre. Dice the butter, put it into a saucepan with water and bring to the boil. Pour the liquid all at once into the flour and mix together quickly; beat until smooth. At first the pastry will be too soft to handle but as it cools it may be rolled out $\frac{1}{8}$–$\frac{1}{4}$ inch (2.5–5 mm) thick, to fit the two tins. The pastry may be made into individual pies or one large pie. Keep back one-third of the pastry for lids.

Fill the pastry-lined tins with the meat mixture which should be almost, but not quite, cooked and cooled a little. Brush the edges of the pastry with the water and egg wash and put on the pastry lids, pinching them tightly together. Roll out the trimmings to make pastry leaves or twirls to decorate the tops of the pies; make a hole in the centre, egg-wash the lid and then egg-wash the decoration also.

Bake the pies for 40 minutes approx. at 200°C/400°F/regulo 6. Serve with a good Green Salad (see page 60).

Lamb with Tomato and Haricot Beans

Serves 8

Hearty lamb, tomato and bean casseroles are a great favourite in France.

4 tablesp. ($\frac{1}{4}$ cup) olive oil
8 ozs (225 g) haricot beans
8 ozs (225 g) streaky bacon, cut into $\frac{1}{2}$ inch (1 cm) cubes
2 cloves of garlic
10 ozs (285 g/2 cups) sliced onions
9 oz (275 g) carrots
4 sticks celery

2 lbs (900 g) lamb, leg *or* shoulder
1 tin of tomatoes *or* 1 lb (450 g) very ripe tomatoes (peeled)
salt, freshly ground pepper and sugar
a bouquet garni made up of a sprig of thyme, several sprigs of parsley, a large sprig of rosemary

Garnish
2 tablesp. chopped parsley

Soak the beans in plenty of cold water overnight. Next day heat the olive oil in a casserole, add the bacon and fry until crisp. Add the mashed garlic and onions, toss for a minute or two, then add the diced carrots and celery, cover and sweat for a few minutes.

Meanwhile cut the lamb into 1½ inch (4 cm) cubes; toss in a little olive oil in a hot pan until the meat changes colour, add to the vegetables with the chopped tomatoes and drained beans. Season with salt, freshly ground pepper and sugar. Add the bouquet of herbs, bring to the boil, cover and simmer for 1–1½ hours depending on the age of the lamb. Taste, correct the seasoning, remove the banquet garni and serve in an earthenware dish. Sprinkle with chopped parsley.

Italian Beef Stew

Serves 6-8

1 tablesp. olive oil	8 fl ozs (250 ml/1 cup) Brown
3 lbs (1.35 kg) well-hung stewing	Beef Stock (see *Simply*
beef *or* lean flank	*Delicious*, page 46)
2 large carrots cut into ½ inch	8 fl ozs (250 ml/1 cup) home-
(1 cm) slices	made Tomato Purée
10 ozs (285 g/2 cups) sliced	5 ozs (140 g/1¼ cups) sliced
onions	mushrooms
1 heaped tablesp. flour	1 tablesp. chopped parsley
8 fl ozs (250 ml/1 cup) red wine	

Trim the meat of any excess fat, then prepare the vegetables. Cut the meat into 1½ inch (4 cm) cubes. Heat the olive oil in a casserole; sweat the sliced onions and carrots on a gentle heat with the lid on for 10 minutes. Heat a little more olive oil in a frying pan until almost smoking. Sear the pieces of meat on all sides, reduce the heat, stir in flour; cook for 1 minute; mix the wine, stock and Tomato Purée together and add gradually to the casserole. Cook gently for 2½–3 hours in a low oven, depending on the cut of meat, 160°C/325°F/regulo 3. Meanwhile sauté the mushrooms and add to the casserole with the parsley, 30 minutes approx. before the end of cooking. Serve with potatoes or noodles and a good green salad.

Tomato Purée

2 lbs (900 g) very ripe tomatoes
1 small onion, chopped
2 teasp. sugar
a good pinch of salt and a few
  twists of black pepper

Cut the tomatoes into quarters; put into a stainless steel saucepan with the onion, salt, freshly ground pepper and sugar. Cook on a gentle heat until the tomatoes are soft (no water is needed). Put through the fine blade of the mouli-legume or a nylon sieve. Allow to get cold, then refrigerate or freeze.

Note: Tomato Purée is one of the very best ways of preserving the flavour of ripe, summer tomatoes for winter. Use for soups, stews, casseroles, etc.

Beef with Murphy

Serves 6–8

Use your favourite stout for this recipe: even Cork people have divided allegiances!

2 lbs (900 g) lean stewing beef,
    e.g. chuck
seasoned flour
3 tablesp. (45 ml) olive oil
2 thinly sliced onions
2 teasp. sugar
1 teasp. dry English mustard
1 tablesp. concentrated tomato
    purée

1 strip of dried orange peel
a bouquet garni made up of 1
    bay leaf, 1 sprig of fresh
    thyme, 4 parsley stalks
1 pint (600 ml/2$\frac{1}{2}$ cups) Murphy
8 ozs (225 g) mushrooms
$\frac{1}{2}$ oz (15 g/$\frac{1}{8}$ stick) butter
salt and freshly ground pepper

Cut the meat into 1$\frac{1}{2}$ inch (4 cm) cubes and toss in seasoned flour. Heat some oil in a hot pan and fry the meat in batches until it is brown on all sides. Transfer the meat into a casserole and add a little more oil to the pan. Fry the thinly-sliced onions until nicely browned; de-glaze with the stout. Add sugar, mustard, tomato purée, orange rind and bouquet garni. Season with salt and freshly ground pepper. Bring to the boil, cover and simmer in a very low oven, 150°C/300°F/regulo 2, for 2–2$\frac{1}{2}$ hours or until the meat is tender.

Meanwhile, wash and slice the mushrooms. Sauté in a very little melted butter in a hot pan. Season with salt and freshly ground pepper. Set aside. When the stew is cooked, add the mushrooms and simmer for 2 to 3 minutes, taste and correct the seasoning. Serve sprinkled with chopped parsley.

Note: This stew reheats well. Some stouts taste a little more 'bitter' than Murphy, so if you are using an alternative brand, you may need to add more sugar to the recipe.

Pan-grilled Steak with Béarnaise Sauce and Pommes Allumettes

Serves 6

Of all the sauces to serve with steak, Béarnaise is my absolute favourite. We find a heavy-ridged cast-iron grill pan the best to cook the steaks when you don't need to make a sauce in the pan.

6 x 6 ozs (170 g) sirloin *or* fillet
   steaks
1 clove of garlic

a little olive oil
salt and freshly ground pepper

Béarnaise Sauce (see below)
Pommes Allumettes (see below)

Garnish
fresh watercress (optional)

Prepare the steaks about 1 hour before cooking. Cut a clove of garlic in half; rub both sides of each steak with the cut clove of garlic, grind some black pepper over the steaks and sprinkle on a few drops of olive oil. Turn the steaks in the oil and leave aside. If using sirloin steaks, score the fat at 1 inch (2.5 cm) intervals. Make the Béarnaise Sauce and keep warm. Heat the grill pan, season the steaks with a little salt and put them down onto the hot pan.

The approximate cooking times for *each side* of the steaks are:

	Sirloin	*Fillet*
rare	2 minutes	5 minutes
medium rare	3 minutes	6 minutes
medium	4 minutes	7 minutes
well done	5 minutes	8–9 minutes

Turn a sirloin steak over onto the fat and cook for 1–2 minutes or until the fat becomes crisp. Put the steaks onto a plate and leave them rest for a few minutes in a warm place while you cook the Pommes Allumettes.

To serve: Put the steaks on hot plates. Serve the Béarnaise Sauce over one end of the steak or in a little bowl on the side of the plate. Garnish with Pommes Allumettes and fresh watercress.

51

Béarnaise Sauce

One of the great classics! Use French rather than Russian tarragon if you can find it.

4 tablesp. ($\frac{1}{4}$ cup) tarragon
  vinegar
4 tablesp. ($\frac{1}{4}$ cup) dry white wine
2 teasp. finely chopped shallots
a pinch of freshly ground pepper
1 tablesp. freshly chopped
  French tarragon leaves

2 egg yolks (preferably
  free-range)
4–6 ozs (110–150 g/1–1$\frac{1}{2}$ sticks)
  butter approx., salted or
  unsalted depending on what it
  is being served with

If you do not have tarragon vinegar to hand, use a wine vinegar and add some extra chopped tarragon. Boil the first four ingredients together until completely reduced and the pan is almost dry but not browned. Add 1 tablespoon of cold water immediately. Pull the pan off the heat and allow to cool for 1 or 2 minutes; whisk in the egg yolks and add the butter bit by bit over a very low heat, whisking all the time. As soon as one piece melts, add the next piece; it will gradually thicken. If it shows signs of becoming too thick or slightly 'scrambling', remove from the heat immediately and add a little cold water if necessary. Do not leave the pan or stop whisking until the sauce is made. Finally add 1 tablespoon of freshly chopped French tarragon and taste for seasoning.

If the sauce is slow to thicken it may be because you are excessively cautious and the heat is too low. Increase the heat slightly and continue to whisk until the sauce thickens to a coating consistency. It is important to remember, however, that if you are making Béarnaise Sauce in a saucepan directly over the heat, it should be possible to put your hand on the side of the saucepan at any stage. If the saucepan feels too hot for your hand it is also too hot for the sauce.

Another good tip if you are making Béarnaise Sauce for the first time is to keep a bowl of cold water close by so that you can plunge the bottom of the saucepan into it if it becomes too hot.

Keep the sauce warm in a bowl over warm water or in a thermos flask until you want to serve it.

Pommes Allumettes

Serves 6

Pommes Allumettes are matchstick potatoes. They are particularly delicious cooked in olive oil.

1 lb (450 g) 'old' potatoes, e.g. Golden Wonders *or* Kerrs Pinks	olive oil for deep-fat frying salt

Wash and peel the potatoes. Cut them into tiny, even matchsticks and soak in cold water for 15 minutes. This will remove the excess starch and prevent the potatoes from sticking together. Dry them thoroughly with a tea-towel.

Heat the oil, 190°C/375°F. Fry the potatoes until they are golden brown and very crisp. Drain on kitchen paper. Sprinkle with salt and serve.

Note: If the Pommes Allumettes are very crisp they will keep in the oven for 10 minutes or even longer.

Supper Dishes

Knowing how busy most people are, I decided to select for this book a few light and delicious dishes which can be put together quickly, often using recipes given earlier in a new or different way. When you simply don't feel like a full three-course meal, or don't have time to cook one, this is the section to turn to. *Real* fast food! All you need are a few basic ideas—and a few left-overs in your fridge.

Pasta with Bacon and Tomato Fondue and Pasta with Piperonata and Bacon use mainstay recipes from the vegetable section, with the addition of a bit of bacon for extra panache and a sprinkling of grated cheese. Both are delicious and take only as long to make as your pasta takes to boil.

Baked Eggs are wonderfully fast, too, and infinitely versatile. They can be absolutely plain as in the basic recipe, or can be transformed with a tablespoon of Tomato Fondue, Piperonata, cooked mushrooms, diced ham or smoked salmon into a stylish starter. Provided the addition isn't of a fleshy nature, Baked Eggs can also be a splendid vegetarian dish.

Scotch Eggs are precisely the sort of slightly out of vogue thing I love to resurrect so that everybody can discover how delicious they can be. With just a piece of pickle or a spoonful of Easy Tomato Chutney (page 74) they make a very tempting supper dish and are delicious for picnics. Ham and Leeks au Gratin, in which leeks are wrapped in a bit of ham or bacon, covered with Béchamel sauce (which by now you can make like a dream!), and topped with crusty buttered crumbs are also a great favourite. Chicory, with its slightly bitter flavour, can be served in exactly the same way.

Pasta with Bacon and Tomato Fondue

Serves 6-8

Here is an example of how versatile Tomato Fondue is.

1 lb (450 g) spaghetti
a dash of oil
1 oz (30 g/¼ stick) butter
salt and freshly ground pepper
Tomato Fondue (see page 67)
8 ozs (225 g) cooked bacon *or*
   ham

4 ozs (110 g/scant 1½ cups) freshly
   grated cheese, e.g. Cheddar *or*
   Parmesan
2 tablesp. fresh basil *or* parsley
   chopped

Bring a large saucepan of water to the boil, add 2 teaspoons of salt and a dash of oil. Add in the spaghetti, stir, boil furiously until almost cooked—*al dente*—15 minutes approx. Meanwhile heat the tomato fondue, add the diced cooked ham or bacon and simmer for 3 or 4 minutes. As soon as the spaghetti is cooked, pour off all the water and drain well; toss in a little butter and season with freshly ground pepper. Pour into a wide, hot bowl or pasta dish, then pour over the tomato fondue. Sprinkle with herbs and grated cheese and serve immediately on very hot plates.

Pasta with Piperonata and Bacon

Follow the recipe for Pasta with Bacon and Tomato Fondue above, but substitute Piperonata for Tomato Fondue. Use half the Piperonata recipe (see page 61).

Baked Eggs and Variations

Serves 4

These may be served as a starter or snack and there are infinite variations on the theme.

4 fresh eggs (preferably
   free-range)
½ oz (15 g/⅛ stick) butter

6–8 tablesp. cream
salt and freshly ground pepper

4 small ramekins (see glossary)

Lightly butter the 4 ramekins. Heat the cream; when it is hot, spoon about 1 tablespoon into each ramekin and break an egg into the cream. Season with salt and freshly ground pepper. Spoon the remainder of the cream over the top of the eggs. Place the ramekins in a bain-marie of hot water, cover with tin foil or a lid and bring to simmering point on top of the stove. Continue to cook either gently on top of the stove, or in a moderate oven, 180°C/350°F/regulo 4, 12 minutes approx. for a soft egg, 15 minutes for a medium egg and 18–20 minutes for a hard egg. Serve immediately.

Baked Eggs with Cheese

Sprinkle $\frac{1}{2}$–1 tablespoon of finely grated cheese on top of each egg. Bake uncovered in a bain-marie in the oven if preferred.

Baked Eggs with Tomato Fondue

Put 1 tablespoon of Tomato Fondue (see page 67) underneath each egg in the ramekins. Proceed as in the basic recipe, with or without the addition of cheese.

Baked Eggs with Piperonata

Put 1 tablespoon of Piperonata (see page 61) underneath each egg in the ramekins. Spoon 1 tablespoon of cream over each egg. Sprinkle $\frac{1}{2}$–1 tablespoon of finely grated cheese on top of each egg; a little cooked bacon or crispy rasher may also be added. Bake uncovered in a bain-marie in the oven if preferred.

Baked Eggs with Smoked Salmon or Smoked Mackerel

Put 1 tablespoon of chopped smoked salmon or flaked smoked mackerel in the base of each ramekin. Add 1–2 tablespoons ($\frac{1}{4}$ oz/$\frac{1}{4}$ cup) of chopped parsley to the cream and proceed as in the basic recipe.

Baked Eggs with Fresh Herbs and Dijon Mustard

Use 3 tablespoons in total of parsley, tarragon, chives and chervil. Mix 2 teaspoons of mustard and 3 tablespoons of freshly chopped herbs into the cream and proceed as for the basic recipe.

Scotch Eggs

Serves 6

An old-fashioned recipe, great for a snack or picnic food. Serve hot or cold.

1 lb (450 g) best-quality sausagemeat	1 beaten egg
	seasoned flour
6 hard-boiled eggs (preferably free-range)	dry, white breadcrumbs
	best-quality oil for deep frying

Bring a saucepan of water to the boil and put in the eggs carefully, one by one. Bring back to the boil and simmer for 10 minutes. (The eggs should be covered with water.) Pour off the water and cover with cold water. Divide the sausagemeat into 6 even-sized pieces. Put a piece of sausagemeat onto a floured board and flatten it with your hand into an oval shape, large enough to cover an egg. Shape the sausagemeat around the peeled egg with your hands, making sure that the egg is evenly coated and there are no cracks. Cover the rest of the eggs in the same way.

Roll the Scotch Eggs in seasoned flour, beaten egg and finally coat them with dry, white breadcrumbs. Coat all the eggs in the same way. Heat the oil for deep frying, making sure it is deep enough to cover the eggs. The fat should be a medium heat, 180°C/350°F, because if it is too hot, the outside will be brown before the inside is cooked. Put the Scotch Eggs into the basket (a few at a time) and lower them into the fat. Fry them for 5 or 6 minutes, then lift them out of the pan and drain on kitchen paper.

Serve hot or cold with a good Green Salad and perhaps a Tomato and Basil Salad (see pages 60 and 13 respectively).

Ham and Leeks au Gratin

Serves 8

Follow the recipe for Leeks Mornay (see page 65), but use 8 slices of cooked ham or bacon. Wrap the cooked ham around each leek before they are arranged side by side in the serving dish. Coat with the Mornay sauce.

Vegetables

Every year more and more people buy a few tomato plants at their local garden centre, bring them home, plant them and look after them all summer long—yet it is about 3 to $3\frac{1}{2}$ months before they get a single fruit. Why go to all that bother—watering, feeding and side-shooting— you might wonder, when you could just pop into a shop and buy what you need? Well, if you taste a home-grown tomato fully ripened on the plant you'll understand why: the flavour is sweet and intense and worth every minute of the hard work. Commercial growers need to pick off their tomatoes green or semi-green to allow for distribution and shelf life, so the fruit ripens in the box and never quite develops that sun-ripened flavour. Irish tomatoes are wonderful in summer, but in winter it can be very difficult to find a tomato with flavour.

Something else that bothers me is the EC grading system, which I know was introduced for the most noble reasons. Growers are required to grade their fruit and vegetables, and quite rightly so, but as a result only 'standard' sizes find their way into the shops. This means that small tomatoes, tiny onions or apples are difficult to find, although often they are the ones with the best flavour. I think we should at least be offered the choice.

Only the very dark red, ripe tomatoes have enough flavour for soups, stews, sauces and dishes, such as Tomato Fondue—a quick and deliciously juicy vegetable recipe which goes wonderfully well with roast or grilled meat but can also be used as a sauce for pasta dishes (page 55), a base for Baked Eggs (page 55) or a filling for omelettes, pancakes or vol-au-vents. Both this and Piperonata are two marvellous stand-bys to have in your fridge. They re-heat perfectly, unlike most vegetables, which suffer if they are cooked at the last moment.

My recipe for cooking leeks usually converts even the most determined sceptic—toss them in a little butter and braise them in a covered casserole. This method works very well with parsnips, globe artichokes and cucumber as well, so if you've looked on cucumber only as a salad vegetable until now, try hot Cucumber with Fennel: there's a new treat in store. You can serve it also as an accompaniment to fish, and with mint as the ideal partner for lamb.

I've also included two traditional Irish potato recipes because these lovely homely dishes have a soft spot in my heart. My mother used to make Colcannon for us every Friday when we ran home up the hill from school for lunch and I still think it's comfort food at its best. The Ulster Champ recipe I've just come across recently—Deborah Shorley, a friend from Ulster who has a great knowledge of traditional food, particularly the food of Ulster, introduced me to it and it's absolutely gorgeous, even made with frozen peas in winter.

You may feel by now that Duchesse Potato is not so much old-fashioned as old hat, since it has appeared in each book I've written so far; but I must include it again because it is a vital element in so many meals, and if it's piped around the edge, it makes a whole meal in one dish. I think you will agree it deserves its space.

Green Salad with Honey Dressing

Green Salad has been included in all my books because we serve it with every lunch and dinner, varying the dressing to suit the menu. For this one, use delicious Irish grainy mustard, for example, the Lake Shore mustard flavoured with honey made by Hilary Henry on the shores of Lough Derg.

a selection of lettuces and salad leaves, e.g. butterhead, iceberg, cos, oakleaf (green *or* bronze), Chinese leaves, lollo rosso, raddichio trevisano,

rocket, salad burnet, golden marjoram *or* edible chrysanthemum leaves and edible flowers

Honey Dressing
12 fl oz (350 g/1$\frac{1}{2}$ cups) approx. virgin olive oil
3 fl ozs (90 ml/scant $\frac{1}{2}$ cup) cider vinegar

1 tablesp. Irish whole grain mustard *or* moutarde de Meaux
a clove of garlic, crushed
1 teasp. pure Irish honey

Makes $\frac{3}{4}$ pint approx.

Wash and dry very carefully the lettuces, salad leaves and flowers. Tear into bite-sized pieces and put into a deep salad bowl. Cover with cling-film and refrigerate, if not to be served immediately.

Meanwhile, make the Dressing. Mix all the ingredients together, whisking well before use. Just before serving, toss the leaves with a little Dressing—just enough to make the leaves glisten. Serve immediately.

Note: Green Salad must not be dressed until just before serving, otherwise it will look tired and unappetising.

Cucumber with Fennel

Serves 4–6

Many people love cucumber raw, but few think of cooking it as a vegetable. It is quite delicious prepared in this way and particularly good with fish.

1 oz (30 g/$\frac{1}{4}$ stick) butter
1 cucumber, peeled

$\frac{1}{2}$ teasp. snipped fresh fennel
salt and freshly ground pepper

Dice the cucumber into $\frac{1}{2}$ inch (1 cm) pieces. Melt the butter in a heavy saucepan or casserole, toss in the cucumber and season with salt and freshly ground pepper. Cover and sweat over a *low* heat until just soft, 20 minutes approx. Stir occasionally. Add some snipped fresh fennel. Taste and correct the seasoning if necessary.

(Cucumber may be cut into dice, rounds or turned in barrel shapes.)

Piperonata*

Serves 8–10

This Italian vegetable stew reheats perfectly and is a valuable stand-by to have in your fridge.

1 onion	2 tablesp. ($\frac{1}{8}$ cup) olive oil
2 red peppers	salt, freshly ground pepper and
2 green peppers	sugar
6 large tomatoes (dark red and very ripe)	a clove of garlic
	a few leaves of fresh basil

Peel the garlic and make into a paste. Peel and slice the onion. Heat 2 tablespoons ($\frac{1}{8}$ cup) of olive oil in a casserole, add the garlic and cook for a few seconds; then add the sliced onion, toss in the oil and allow to soften over a gentle heat in a covered casserole while the peppers are being prepared. Halve the peppers, remove the seeds carefully, cut into quarters and then into strips across rather than lengthways. Add to the onion and toss in the oil; replace the lid and continue to cook.

Meanwhile peel the tomatoes (scald in boiling water for 10 seconds, pour off the water and peel immediately). Slice the tomatoes and add to the casserole, season with salt, freshly ground pepper, sugar and a few leaves of fresh basil if available. Cook until the vegetables are just soft, 30 minutes approx. Serve with bacon, ham, beef, monkfish, lamb etc., or as a filling for omelettes. Piperonata will keep in the fridge for 4 or 5 days.

Suggestions for Other Uses

Piperonata may be served as:
1. A filling for omelettes, stuffed pancakes or vol-au-vents;
2. Vegetarian Lasagne (see page 76);
3. A sauce for pasta.

Colcannon*

Serves 8 approx.

This traditional Irish potato recipe is comfort food at its very best.

2½–3 lbs (900 g–1 kg) 'old' potatoes, e.g. **Golden Wonders** *or* **Kerrs Pinks**	8 fl ozs (250 ml/1 cup) approx. boiling milk
1 **Savoy** *or* **spring cabbage**	salt and freshly ground pepper
	2 ozs (55 g/½ stick) approx. butter

Scrub the potatoes and cook them in their jackets. Put them in a saucepan of cold water, add a good pinch of salt and bring to the boil. When the potatoes are about half cooked, 15 minutes approx. for 'old' potatoes, strain off two-thirds of the water, replace the lid on the saucepan, put onto a gentle heat and allow the potatoes to steam until they are cooked.

Remove the dark outer leaves from the cabbage. Wash the rest and cut into quarters, remove the core and cut finely across the grain. Boil in a little boiling salted water or bacon-cooking water until soft. Drain, season with salt, freshly ground pepper and a little butter. When the potatoes are just cooked, put on the milk and bring to the boil. Pull the peel off the potatoes, mash quickly while they are still warm and beat in enough boiling milk to make a fluffy purée. (If you have a large quantity, put the potatoes in the bowl of a food mixer and beat with the spade.) Then stir in the cooked cabbage and taste for seasoning. Cover with tin foil while reheating so it doesn't get crusty on top.

Colcannon may be prepared ahead up to this point and reheated later in a moderate oven, 180°C/350°F/regulo 4, for 20–25 minutes approx.

Serve in a hot dish or with a lump of butter melting in the centre.

Ulster Champ

Serves 8

I am indebted to Deborah Shorley for this recipe, which she calls Claragh Champ; we call it Ulster Champ down here and I prefer to cook the potatoes in their jackets rather than peeling them first.

4 lbs (1.8 kg) 'old' potatoes,
  e.g. Golden Wonders *or*
  Kerrs Pinks
1 lb (450 g/4 cups) young peas,
  shelled weight
8 tablesp. (1 cup) chopped
  parsley

1 pint (600 ml/2½ cups) milk
salt and freshly ground pepper
2–4 ozs (55–110 g/½-1 stick) butter
  (traditionally, strong country
  butter would have been used)

Cook the potatoes in boiling salted water until tender; drain well, dry over the heat in the pan for a few minutes, peel and mash with most of the butter while hot. Meanwhile bring the milk to the boil and simmer the peas until just cooked, 8–10 minutes approx. Add the parsley for the final 2 minutes of cooking. Add the hot milk mixture to the potatoes. Season well, beat until creamy and smooth and serve piping hot with a lump of butter melting in the centre.

Duchesse Potato

Serves 4

2 lb (900 g) unpeeled 'old'
  potatoes, e.g. Golden Wonders
  or Kerrs Pinks
½ pint (300 ml/10 fl ozs) creamy
  milk

1–2 egg yolks *or* 1 whole egg and
  1 egg yolk (preferably
  free-range)
1–2 ozs (30–55 g/¼-½ stick) butter

Scrub the potatoes well. Put them into a saucepan of cold water, add a good pinch of salt and bring to the boil. When the potatoes are about half cooked, 15 minutes approx. for 'old' potatoes, strain off two-thirds of the water, replace the lid on the saucepan, put onto a gentle heat and allow the potatoes to steam until they are cooked.

Peel immediately by just pulling off the skins, so you have as little waste as possible; mash while hot (see note below). (If you have a large quantity, put the potatoes into the bowl of a food mixer and beat with the spade.)

While the potatoes are being peeled, bring approx. ½ pint (300 ml) of milk to the boil. Beat the eggs into the hot mashed potatoes, and add enough boiling creamy milk to mix to a soft light consistency suitable for piping; then beat in the butter, the amount depending on how rich you like your potatoes. Taste and season with salt and freshly ground pepper.

Note: If the potatoes are not peeled and mashed while hot and if the boiling milk is not added immediately, the Duchesse Potato will be lumpy and gluey.

If you only have egg whites they will be fine and will make a delicious light mashed potato also.

Buttered Leeks*

Serves 4–6

Many people dislike leeks, I think possibly because they have only had them boiled. Try them this way—they are meltingly tender and mild in flavour.

4 medium-sized leeks	1 tablesp. water if necessary
1½ ozs (45 g/generous ¼ stick) butter	salt and freshly ground pepper
	chopped parsley *or* chervil

Cut off the dark green leaves from the top of the leeks (wash and add to the stock pot or use for making green leek soup). Slit the leeks about half way down the centre and wash well under cold running water. Slice into ¼ inch (5 mm) rounds. Melt the butter in a heavy saucepan; when it foams, add the sliced leeks and toss gently to coat with butter. Season with salt and freshly ground pepper and add 1 tablesp. water if necessary. Cover with a paper lid and a close-fitting saucepan lid. Reduce the heat and cook very gently for 20–30 minutes approx., or until soft and moist. Check and stir every now and then. Serve on a warm dish sprinkled with chopped parsley or chervil.

Note: The pot of leeks may be cooked in the oven if that is more convenient, 160°C/325°F/regulo 3.

Dingle Pie

Colcannon

Provençale Bean Stew

Ballymaloe Cheese Fondue

Leeks Mornay

Serves 8

8 medium-sized leeks
1 pint (600 ml/2½ cups) milk
a few slices of carrot and onion
3 or 4 peppercorns
a sprig of thyme or parsley
roux (see glossary)
5–6 ozs (140–170 g/1¼-1½ cups)
  grated Cheddar cheese or 3 ozs
  (85 g/¾ cup) grated Parmesan
  cheese

¼ teasp. mustard, preferably
  Dijon
salt and freshly ground pepper
Buttered Crumbs (see page 24)
  (optional)

Trim most of the green part off the leeks (use in the stock pot). Leave the white parts whole, slit the top and wash well under cold running water. Cook in a little boiling salted water in a covered saucepan until just tender, 15 minutes approx.

Meanwhile put the cold milk into a saucepan with a few slices of carrot and onion, 3 or 4 peppercorns and a sprig of thyme or parsley. Bring to the boil, simmer for 5 minutes, remove from heat and leave to infuse for 10 minutes. Strain out the vegetables, bring the milk back to the boil and thicken with roux to a light coating consistency. Add the mustard and two-thirds of the grated cheese, but keep the remainder of the cheese for sprinkling over the top. Season with salt and freshly ground pepper, taste and correct the seasoning if necessary.

Drain the leeks well, arrange in a serving dish, coat with the sauce and sprinkle with grated cheese mixed with a few Buttered Crumbs (if you have them to hand, see page 24). Reheat in a moderate oven, 180°F/ regulo 4, until golden and bubbly.

Cauliflower Cheese

Serves 6-8

1 medium-sized cauliflower with green leaves	**salt**

Mornay Sauce

1 pint (600 ml/2$\frac{1}{2}$ cups) milk with a dash of cream	**salt and freshly ground pepper**
a slice of onion	**4 ozs (110 g/1 cup) grated cheese,**
3–4 slices of carrot	** e.g. Cheddar** *or* **a mixture of**
6 peppercorns	** Gruyère, Parmesan and**
thyme *or* **parsley**	** Cheddar**
1 oz (30 g/$\frac{1}{4}$ stick) butter	**$\frac{1}{4}$ teasp. mustard**
1 oz (30 g/scant $\frac{1}{4}$ cup) flour	**1 oz (30 g/$\frac{1}{4}$ cup) grated mature**
	** Cheddar cheese for top**

Remove the outer leaves and wash well both the cauliflower and the leaves. Put not more than 1 inch (2.5 cm) of water in a saucepan just large enough to take the cauliflower; add a little salt. Chop the leaves into small pieces and either leave the cauliflower whole or cut in quarters; place the cauliflower on top of the green leaves in the saucepan, cover and simmer until the cauliflower is cooked, 15 minutes approx. Test by piercing the stalk with a knife: there should be just a little resistance. Remove the cauliflower and leaves to an ovenproof serving dish.

Meanwhile make the Mornay Sauce. Put the cold milk into a saucepan with a slice of onion, 3–4 slices of carrot, 6 peppercorns and a sprig of thyme or parsley. Bring to the boil, simmer for 3–4 minutes, remove from the heat and leave to infuse for 10 minutes. Strain out the vegetables, bring the milk back to the boil and thicken with roux to a light coating consistency. Add 4 ozs (110 g/1 cup) grated cheese and a little mustard. Season with salt and freshly ground pepper, taste and correct the seasoning if necessary. Spoon the sauce over the cauliflower and sprinkle with more grated cheese. The dish may be prepared ahead to this point.

Put into a hot oven, 230°C/450°F/regulo 8, or under the grill to brown. If the Cauliflower Cheese is allowed to get completely cold, it will take 20–25 minutes to reheat in a moderate oven, 180°C/350°F/regulo 4.

Serve sprinkled with chopped parsley.

Note: If the cauliflower is left whole, cut a deep cross in the stalk.

Buttered Cabbage*

Serves 6–8

The flavour of cabbage cooked in this quick way is often a revelation to people when they taste it.

1 lb (450 g) fresh Savoy cabbage
1–2 ozs (30–55 g/$\frac{1}{4}$–$\frac{1}{2}$ stick) butter

salt and freshly ground pepper
a knob of butter

Remove the tough outer leaves from the cabbage. Divide into four, cut out the stalks and then cut into fine shreds across the grain. Put 2 or 3 tablespoons of water into a wide saucepan with the butter and a pinch of salt. Bring to the boil, add the cabbage and toss constantly over a high heat; cover for a few minutes. Toss again and add some salt, freshly ground pepper and the knob of butter. Serve immediately.

Tomato Fondue*

Serves 6 approx.

This wonderful tomato stew, literally 'melted tomatoes', is best made during the summer months when tomatoes are very ripe.

2 lbs (900 g) very ripe tomatoes
4 ozs (110 g/1 cup) sliced onions
a clove of garlic, crushed
 (optional)
1 dessertsp. oil

1 tablesp. of any of the
 following, chopped: thyme,
 parsley, mint, basil, lemon
 balm, marjoram
salt, freshly ground pepper and
 sugar to taste

Sweat the sliced onions and garlic (if used) in oil on a gentle heat. It is vital for the success of this dish that the onions are completely soft before the tomatoes are added. Remove the hard core from the tomatoes. Put them into a deep bowl and cover them with boiling water. Count to 10 and then pour off the water immediately; peel off the skins, slice and add to the onions. Season with salt, freshly ground pepper and sugar and add a generous sprinkling of chopped herbs: mint or basil are my favourites. Cook for just 5 or 10 minutes more, or until the tomato softens.

Note: This may be served not only as a vegetable but also as a sauce, a filling or a topping for pizza; reduce a little more for a pizza, or it may be too sloppy.

Buttered Courgettes

Serves 4

1 lb (450 g) courgettes, no larger than 5 inches (12.5 cm) in length
1 oz (30 g/¼ stick) butter

a dash of olive oil
salt and freshly ground pepper
freshly chopped parsley

Top and tail the courgettes and cut them into ¼ inch (5 mm) slices. Melt the butter and add a dash of olive oil, toss in the courgettes and coat in the butter and oil. Cook until tender, 4–5 minutes approx. Season with salt and freshly ground pepper. Turn into a hot serving dish, sprinkle with chopped parsley and serve immediately.

Mushroom à la Crème

Serves 4

½–1 oz (15–30 g/⅛–¼ stick) butter
3 ozs (85 g/¾ cup) finely chopped onion
½ lb (225 g/2¼ cups) sliced mushrooms
4 fl ozs (100 ml/½ cup) cream

½ tablesp. chopped chives (optional)
parsley
a squeeze of lemon juice
salt and freshly ground pepper

Melt the butter in a heavy saucepan until it foams. Add the chopped onions, cover and sweat on a gentle heat for 5–10 minutes or until quite soft but not coloured; remove the onions to a bowl. Increase the heat and cook the sliced mushrooms in batches if necessary. Season each batch with salt, freshly ground pepper and a tiny squeeze of lemon juice. Add the onions and chives to the mushrooms in the saucepan, then add the cream and allow to bubble for a few minutes; taste and correct the seasoning.

Note: Mushroom à la Crème may be served as a vegetable, or as a filling for vol-au-vents, bouchées or pancakes. It may also be used as an enrichment for casseroles and stews or, by adding a little more cream or stock, may be served as a sauce with beef, lamb, chicken or veal. A crushed clove of garlic may also be added when the onions are sweating.

Vegetarian Dishes

There is no doubt about it, more and more Irish people are turning to vegetarian or part-vegetarian food—some for moral reasons, some because a wider range of tempting vegetables is available than ever before and some for the good of their health. There is also a general unease about the presence of hormones and antibiotics in meat and the apparent failure to implement strict enough controls to restrict their use, which is unfortunate for those producers whose meat is beyond reproach, and it is very difficult for the consumer to tell which is which. Apart from that, there is a general move away from the meat-laden Irish diet of old with the growing realisation that we don't actually need to eat huge quantities of meat to be healthy.

In tandem with this, vegetarian cooking, which used to have a deadly dull boiled rice and lentils image, has recently become much more adventurous. Many restaurants now offer vegetarian alternatives which are every bit as tempting as the other dishes on the menu—if not more so! So for these reasons I am including a few vegetarian recipes in this book.

I begin with Provençale Bean Stew and Green Lentil and Bean Salad because dried beans and pulses are such a rich and cheap source of protein, making them an indispensable part of a vegetarian diet. They also keep indefinitely. Some were found intact in the Pyramids—but from the cook's point of view this is rather pushing things! The longer they are kept, the drier they become and consequently the longer they take to cook, so it's as well to use them up within a year. For any bean recipes, you have to think ahead, since soaking for eight hours or so is essential. Once the beans are cooked, however, you can freeze them very satisfactorily and so save time the next time.

The other great protein-rich vegetarian mainstay is cheese. We use the delicious mature Irish Cheddar both for cooking and nibbling. It is slightly more expensive and less in evidence than ordinary Cheddar but I feel its nuttier, richer taste makes the quest and the extra cost worthwhile. The mature Irish Cheddar which I buy from my local creamery comes in big 'truckles' wrapped in muslin; it has marvellous flavour for both cooking and eating. It is the basis of the Ballymaloe Cheese Fondue, a recipe to keep up your sleeve for an evening when you get home late and exhausted. With crusty bread dipped in, it's the fastest, most deliciously nutritious meal you could ever hope to find and even more delicious with a glass of wine. Don't just save it to eat on your own: it's great for a party also—but just be careful where you sit. According to fondue tradition, she who drops her bread into the pot must kiss the gentleman on her left! (This could be your great chance to give fate a helping hand!) Fondue parties are always fun and children love them too.

Mature Cheddar also gives its incomparable flavour to the other vegetarian dishes here—Leek, Potato and Cheddar Cheese Pie, Macaroni Cheese (my children's favourite supper dish and it doesn't have to be strictly vegetarian—you can add bits of ham or fried bacon if you like); and Vegetarian Lasagne which uses basic Béchamel (page 20) and Piperonata (page 61).

Many of the Salades Tièdes in Soups and Starters can of course be adapted for vegetarians. Further proof that when you learn one or two techniques you can do any number of wonderful things with them.

Provençale Bean Stew*

Serves 8

This is a delicious rustic bean stew, cheap to make yet wonderfully filling and nutritious, and a particularly good dish for vegetarians. Do not add the salt to the beans until near the end of the cooking time, otherwise they seem to harden.

12 ozs (340 g/2 cups) approx. dried haricot, kidney or black-eyed beans or a mixture of all three
1–3 carrots
1–3 onions
1–3 bouquet garni
salt, freshly ground pepper and sugar
2 tablesp. ($\frac{1}{8}$ cup) virgin olive oil
8 ozs (225 g/4 cups) sliced onions
1 large red pepper, cored, seeded and sliced

1 large green pepper, cored, seeded and sliced
2 cloves of garlic, crushed
1 tin of tomatoes, 14 ozs (397 g) or 1 lb (450 g) peeled, very ripe tomatoes, chopped
2 tablesp. (scant $\frac{1}{4}$ cup) concentrated tomato purée
1 teasp. chopped marjoram, thyme or basil
1 bouquet garni
2 ozs (55 g/$\frac{1}{3}$ cup) black olives
2 tablesp. chopped parsley

The day before cooking, pick over the beans, cover with plenty of cold water and leave overnight (soak each type of bean separately). Next day, drain the beans, place in a saucepan or saucepans and cover with fresh cold water. Add a chunk of carrot, a small onion and a bouquet garni to each pot. Bring to the boil, boil rapidly for 10 minutes, then cover and simmer until almost tender. The cooking time varies according to the variety and age of the beans, so for this reason it is better to cook the beans in separate pots and mix them later. Add a pinch of salt towards the end of cooking.

When the beans are tender but not mushy, strain and reserve 10 fl ozs (300 ml/1$\frac{1}{4}$ cups) of the liquid and discard the vegetables and bouquet garni. Heat the oil in a casserole and sweat the onions on a low heat for 5 minutes approx. Add the peppers and garlic, cover and continue to sweat gently for 10 minutes. Add the tomatoes with their juice, tomato purée, herbs, beans, bouquet garni, reserved cooking liquid, salt, freshly ground pepper and a pinch of sugar. Cover and simmer for 20 minutes approx., or until the beans and peppers are cooked. 5 minutes before the end of cooking time, add the olives and freshly chopped parsley. Remove the bouquet garni, taste and correct the seasoning.

Note: 1 lb (450 g) streaky bacon, blanched and de-rinded, cut into $\frac{1}{2}$ inch (1 cm) cubes may be added to this stew. Brown the cubes in olive oil before adding the peppers. If this bean stew is being eaten without meat, then rice should be eaten in the same meal in order to get maximum food value from the beans.

Plain Boiled Rice*

Serves 8

I find this way of cooking rice in what we call 'unlimited water' to be very satisfactory for plain boiled rice, even, dare I say, foolproof. The grains stay separate and it will keep happily covered in the oven for up to half an hour.

14 ozs (400 g/2 cups) good-quality long-grain rice, e.g. Basmati	a large pot of cold water
	a few little knobs of butter (optional)
1½–2 teasp. salt	

Bring a large saucepan of water to a fast boil, add salt, sprinkle in the rice and stir at once to make sure the grains don't stick. Boil rapidly, uncovered. After 4 or 5 minutes (depending on the type of rice) test by biting a few grains between your teeth—it should still have a slightly resistant core. If it overcooks at this stage the grains will stick together later.

Strain well through a sieve or fine strainer. Put into a warm serving dish, dot with a few knobs of butter, cover with tin foil or a lid and leave in a low oven, 140°C/275°F/regulo 1, for a minimum of 15 minutes. Remove the lid, fluff up with a fork and serve.

Green Lentil and Bean Salad

Serves 8

This salad may be eaten on its own or as part of a selection of salads. Warm crispy bacon or pickled pork is good with it also.

2 ozs (55 g/⅓ cup) haricot beans	3 small carrots
2 ozs (55 g/⅓ cup) kidney beans	3 bouquet garni
2 ozs (55 g/⅓ cup) green lentils	3 small onions, each stuck with 2 cloves

French Dressing
9 fl ozs (275 ml/2¼ cups) extra
  virgin olive oil
3 fl ozs (50 ml/scant ½ cup) red *or*
  white wine vinegar
salt and freshly ground pepper

1 dessertsp. Dijon mustard
1 teasp. chives
3 large cloves of garlic
1 teasp. thyme
1 teasp. parsley

Garnish
2 teasp. freshly chopped parsley

2 teasp. fresh basil

Soak the beans in cold water *separately* overnight. Lentils do not need to be soaked. Cook the pulses in separate saucepans; cover each with 3 cups of cold water and add a carrot, onion and bouquet garni to each saucepan. Do not add salt to the beans until almost cooked. Beans take anything from 20–60 minutes to cook, depending on variety and age. Lentils take 10 minutes approx. They should be soft, but still hold their shape. (Keep the cooking liquids—they may be used as a base for a bean or lentil soup and are full of vitamins.)

Whisk or liquidise ingredients for French Dressing together; it should be very well seasoned and quite sharp. Make sure the pulses are well drained. While they are *still warm*, toss the beans and lentils in the French Dressing, using enough just to coat the pulses. Taste and season well with salt and freshly ground pepper, and fold in the chopped parsley and basil.

Note: This salad must be carefully seasoned, otherwise it will taste bland.

*Ballymaloe Cheese Fondue**

Serves 2

Myrtle Allen devised this Cheese Fondue recipe made from Irish Cheddar cheese. It's a great favourite at Ballymaloe and even though it's a meal in itself it may be made in minutes and is loved by adults and children alike. A fondue set is obviously an advantage but not essential.

2 tablesp. (⅛ cup) white wine
a small clove of garlic, crushed
2 teasp. Easy Tomato Chutney
  (see page 74)

2 teasp. freshly chopped parsley
6 ozs (170 g/2 cups) grated
  mature Cheddar cheese
crusty white bread

Put the white wine and the rest of the ingredients into a small saucepan or fondue pot and stir. Just before serving put over a low heat until the cheese melts and begins to bubble. Put the pot over the fondue stove and serve immediately with fresh French bread or cubes of ordinary white bread crisped up in a hot oven.

Note: Ballymaloe Country Relish (available in shops countrywide) is a delicious alternative to Easy Tomato Chutney.

Easy Tomato Chutney

This is a fast recipe for ripe tomato chutney which may be made in 20–25 minutes approx. It keeps for 1 month or more.

$\frac{1}{2}$ lb (225 g) very ripe tomatoes,
  peeled
$2\frac{1}{2}$ ozs (70 g/$\frac{1}{3}$ cup) sugar
2 ozs (55 g/$\frac{1}{2}$ cup) chopped onion
$\frac{1}{2}$ teasp. salt

a pinch of white pepper
$\frac{1}{4}$ teasp. Dijon mustard
a pinch of pimento *or* allspice
$\frac{1}{4}$ pint (150 ml/generous $\frac{1}{2}$ cup)
  wine vinegar

Put all the ingredients into a blender and reduce to a purée. Transfer the mixture to a stainless steel or enamelled saucepan. Cook and reduce over a low heat for 20 minutes approx., until it becomes very thick ($\frac{1}{2} - \frac{1}{3}$ of its original volume). Pour into a sterilised jar or jars.

Leek, Potato and Cheddar Cheese Pie

Serves 8

A cheap and cheerful winter lunch or supper dish, or indeed it may also be served as a vegetable.

1 lb (450 g/4 cups) leeks
1 lb (450 g/$2\frac{1}{2}$ cups) 'old'
  potatoes, e.g. Golden Wonders
  or Kerrs Pinks
2 ozs (55 g/$\frac{1}{2}$ stick) butter
salt and freshly ground pepper

1 x 2 pint (1.1 L) capacity pie
  dish

1 pint (600 ml/2 cups) Cheddar
  cheese sauce (see Mornay
  Sauce, page 24)
$\frac{1}{2}$ clove of garlic, crushed
2 tablesp. grated cheese

Cook the potatoes in salted boiling water. Cut the green parts off the leeks, wash the white parts well and cut into $\frac{1}{2}$ inch (1 cm) rounds. Melt the butter in a casserole, toss in the leeks, season with salt and freshly ground pepper, cover and cook for 20 minutes on a very low heat. Make the cheese sauce (see Mornay Sauce recipe on page 24) but add a crushed clove of garlic; it should be a light coating consistency. When the potatoes are cooked, peel and cut into $\frac{1}{2}$ inch (1 cm) cubes and mix gently with the leeks and sauce. Turn into a pie dish. Sprinkle with grated Cheddar cheese. This pie may be prepared ahead and reheated later in a moderate oven, 180°C/350°F/regulo 4, until golden and bubbly on top, 20 minutes approx.

Macaroni Cheese

Serves 6

Macaroni Cheese is one of my children's favourite supper dishes. They prefer it without the onion, but I often add some cubes of cooked bacon or ham to the sauce when I'm adding in the macaroni.

8 ozs (225 g/2$\frac{1}{2}$ cups) macaroni
4 pints (2.3 L/10 cups) water
1 teasp. salt
4 ozs (110 g/1 cup) chopped onion *or* spring onion, including green stalks (optional)
2 ozs (55 g/$\frac{1}{2}$ stick) butter
2 ozs (55 g/$\frac{1}{2}$ cup) flour

1$\frac{1}{2}$ pints (900 ml/3$\frac{3}{4}$ cups) boiling milk
$\frac{1}{4}$ teasp. Dijon mustard
1 tablesp. chopped parsley (optional)
salt and freshly ground pepper
4$\frac{1}{4}$ ozs (145 g/1$\frac{1}{2}$ cups) grated mature Cheddar cheese

1 x 2 pint (1.1 L) capacity pie dish

Bring 4 pints (2.3 L/10 cups) of water to the boil with 1 teaspoon of salt. Sprinkle in the macaroni and stir to make sure it doesn't stick together; cook until just soft, 15 minutes approx. Meanwhile melt the butter and sweat the onions gently in it until soft, 8-10 minutes approx. Add in the flour and cook, stirring occasionally for 1-2 minutes. Blend in the milk gradually and bring back to the boil; keep stirring. Add $\frac{1}{4}$ teaspoon of mustard, the parsley, salt and freshly ground pepper to taste, and 2$\frac{1}{2}$ ozs (70 g/generous $\frac{1}{2}$ cup) of the cheese. Stir in the cooked macaroni and turn into a pie dish. Sprinkle the top with the remaining cheese. Reheat in a hot oven, 200°C/400°F/regulo 6, or under the grill until the top is brown and bubbly.

This is good served with cold meat, particularly ham.

Vegetarian Lasagne

Serves 12

1 box (13 ozs /375 g) approx.
plain *or* spinach lasagne
1 × Piperonata recipe (see page
61)
1 × Mushroom à la Crème recipe
(see page 68, make twice the
amount)
1 × Tomato Fondue recipe (see
page 67)

1 large *or* 2 medium-sized
lasagne dishes

3 pints (1.7 L/7½ cups) milk made
into well-seasoned Béchamel
Sauce (not too thick, see page
20)
8 ozs (225 g/2 cups) grated
cheese, Parmesan *or* mature
Cheddar *or* Cheddar and
Parmesan mixed
salt and freshly ground pepper

First taste each component; make sure it is delicious and well seasoned.

Blanch the lasagne as directed on the packet; some of the 'easy cook' lasagne may be used without blanching. Spread a little Béchamel sauce on the base of each dish, cover with strips of lasagne and a layer of piperonata. Next put another layer of lasagne. Spread with Béchamel sauce and sprinkle with grated cheese; add the Mushroom à la Crème next, then more lasagne, Béchamel sauce, cheese, Tomato Fondue, another layer of lasagne and so on. (See resumé at end of recipe.) Finally cover with a layer of sauce and a good sprinkling of Parmesan cheese. (Make sure all the lasagne is under the sauce.)

Bake in a moderate oven, 180°C/350°F/regulo 4, for 30 minutes approx. or until golden and bubbly on top. If possible, leave to stand for 10–15 minutes before cutting to allow the layers to compact. Serve with a good green salad.

Resumé
1. Béchamel sauce
2. Lasagne
3. Piperonata
4. Lasagne
5. Béchamel sauce
6. Cheese
7. Mushroom à la Crème
8. Lasagne
9. Béchamel sauce
10. Cheese
11. Tomato Fondue
12. Lasagne
13. Béchamel sauce
14. Cheese

Cabbage, Pineapple and Onion Salad

Serves 6

This salad would use up the tinned pineapple left over after you have used the juice for glazing bacon. It is quite delicious with meat, particularly ham, bacon or pork.

$\frac{1}{2}$ small Savoy cabbage, 12 ozs (340 g) approx.
$\frac{1}{2}$ tin of pineapple (15 ozs/425 g)
1 small onion (3 ozs/85 g/ generous $\frac{1}{2}$ cup) very finely sliced into onion rings

2 tablesp. chopped parsley
salt, freshly ground pepper and sugar

French Dressing
3 tablesp. sunflower oil
3 tablesp. olive oil
2 tablesp. ($\frac{1}{8}$ cup) white wine vinegar

a clove of garlic
$\frac{1}{4}$ teasp. mustard
salt and freshly ground pepper

Cut the cabbage into quarters; cut out the hard core and slice into very thin shreds across the grain. Put into a salad bowl. Cut the pineapple into chunks and add to the cabbage with the very finely sliced onion rings and 1 tablespoon of chopped parsley. Toss in French Dressing, season with salt, freshly ground pepper and sugar. Sprinkle the rest of the parsley on top.

Serve with cold ham or bacon.

Puddings

As elsewhere in the book and the television series that goes with it, I've based some of the recipes in this section on a couple of very useful techniques and added in other favourites chosen either because they are a little bit different or for quite the opposite reason: because they are perennially popular.

Many people seem to have a mental block about using gelatine. I demonstrate in one programme a foolproof method for dealing with it, and include here several other recipes for gelatine-based desserts. It may seem odd that some are termed mousses and others soufflés; the difference is often simply one of aesthetics: in a cold soufflé, a band of paper is tied around the dish and the mousse mixture poured in above the level of the rim to give the appearance of a risen soufflé.

Caramel is another very useful technique that causes quite unnecessary anxiety. Once you master it, it can be used in a mousse, an ice-cream or a Crème Caramel, or as a sauce. The Orange Caramel Cream is a more extravagant version of this—lovely for a special occasion.

Fruit puddings are always popular for their lightness. Room can usually be found for something fruity and delicious, even after the most gargantuan repast. Three of the fruit-based recipes I've chosen use limes which add an exotic touch without being impossibly difficult to track down. In each case, they make a marvellously sophisticated and clean-tasting dessert. But you mustn't be tempted to serve whipped cream with any of them! It simply doesn't go well with the zingy, palate-cleansing quality limes bring to these puddings.

Whipped cream addicts need not fear, however: cream is a must with the two old-fashioned puddings here, Country Rhubarb Cake and Peter Lamb's Apple Charlotte—and don't forget to sprinkle them with a little of my favourite soft brown sugar. The Chocolate Meringue Gâteau is a totally decadent and absolutely scrumptious sandwich filled with rich rum and chocolate-flavoured cream. I can't think of a better thing to finish with. This is the sort of pudding everybody will greedily devour while they moan about their waistlines. Then they'll ask for more—and not regret a single crumb!

Orange Mousse with Chocolate Wafers*

Serves 6–8

2 oranges (1½ if very large)
4 eggs (preferably free-range)
2¼ ozs (70 g/generous ¼ cup)
  castor sugar
½ oz (15 g/2 American ˙ican
  teasp.) gelatine

3 tablesp. water
1 lemon
8 fl ozs (250 ml/1 cup) whipped
  cream

Chocolate Wafers
2 ozs (55 g) best-quality dark
  chocolate

Decoration
2 oranges
8 fl ozs (250 ml/1 cup) whipped
  cream

a pinch of castor sugar

Wash and dry the oranges; grate the rind on the finest part of a stainless steel grater. Put into a bowl with 2 eggs, 2 egg yolks and the castor sugar. Whisk to a thick mousse, preferably with an electric mixer. Put 3 tablespoons of water in a little bowl, measure the gelatine carefully and sprinkle over the water. Leave to 'sponge' for a few minutes until the gelatine has soaked up the water and feels spongy to the touch. Put the bowl into a saucepan of simmering water and allow the gelatine to dissolve completely. All the granules should be dissolved and it should look perfectly clear.

Meanwhile, squeeze the juice from the 2 oranges and 1 lemon, measure and if necessary bring up to ½ pint (300 ml/1¼ cups) with water. Stir a little of the juice into the gelatine and then mix well with the remainder of the juice. Gently stir this into the mousse; cool in the fridge, *stirring regularly*. When the mousse is just beginning to set around the edges, fold in the softly whipped cream. Whisk the 2 egg whites stiffly and fold in gently. Pour into a glass bowl or into individual bowls. Allow to set for 3–4 hours in the fridge.

Meanwhile make the chocolate wafers. Melt the chocolate in a bowl over barely simmering water. Stir until quite smooth. Spread on a flat piece of heavy, white notepaper or light card. Put into a cold place until stiff enough to cut in square or diamond shapes.

While the chocolate is setting, make the orange-flavoured cream. Grate the rind from half an orange, add to the cream and add a pinch of castor sugar to taste. Peel and segment the oranges. Decorate the top of the mousse with orange segments and pipe on some rosettes of orange-flavoured cream. Peel the chocolate wafers off the card and use them to decorate the edges of the mousse.

Chocolate Meringue Gâteau

Serves 6

2 egg whites	**2 rounded teasp. cocoa powder**
4½ ozs (125 g/1⅛ cups) icing sugar	

Chocolate and Rum Cream

1 oz (30 g) best-quality dark chocolate	**½ pint (300 ml/1¼ cups) softly whipped cream**
½ oz (15 g) unsweetened chocolate	**1 tablesp. Jamaican rum**
	1 tablesp. cream

Preheat the oven to 150°C/300°F/regulo 2.

Mark two 7½ inches (19 cm) circles on silicone paper on a prepared baking sheet.

Check that the bowl is dry, spotlessly clean and free of grease. Put the egg whites into the bowl and add 4 ozs (110 g/1 cup) icing sugar all at once; whisk until the mixture forms stiff, dry peaks, 10 minutes approx. Sieve together the cocoa and the remaining ½ oz (15 g) icing sugar and fold in very gently. Spread and bake immediately in the preheated oven for 45 minutes or until just crisp. Allow to get completely cold then peel off the paper.

Meanwhile, very gently melt the chocolate with the rum and 1 tablespoon of cream in a very cool oven, or in a bowl over simmering water. Cool and then fold the mixture into the softly whipped cream; don't stir too much or it may curdle.

Sandwich the two meringue discs together with Chocolate and Rum Cream and decorate with chocolate wafers (see page 79).

Orange Mousse with Chocolate Wafers

Bananas with Lime and Orange Zest

Lemon Soufflé

Crème Caramel

Lemon Soufflé

Serves 6–8

3 large eggs (preferably
  free-range)
8 ozs (225 g/1 cup) castor sugar
2½ lemons
10 fl ozs (300 ml/1¼ cups) cream

½ oz (15 g/3 rounded teasp.)
  gelatine
2½ fl ozs (60 ml/generous ¼ cup)
  water
oil

Decoration
5 fl ozs (150 ml/generous ½ cup)
  whipped cream
2 tablesp. toasted chopped
  almonds

tiny sprigs of lemon balm *or*
  sweet geranium leaves

Brush a collar of greaseproof paper lightly with a tasteless oil; tie it around a 6 inch (15 cm) soufflé bowl. Grate the rind of the lemon and squeeze and strain its juice; separate the eggs and put the yolks, castor sugar, grated lemon rind and strained lemon juice into a bowl. Place the bowl in a saucepan of barely simmering water, then whisk the mixture until quite thick and mousse-like. Remove from the heat and continue whisking until the bowl is cold. If you are using an electric food mixer, whisk the egg yolks, castor sugar and lemon rind until thick. Heat the lemon juice, add and continue to whisk until the mousse reaches the 'ribbon' stage, 15 minutes approx.

Whip the cream softly and fold into the mixture. Sponge the gelatine with the water in a small bowl. Put the bowl into a saucepan of simmering water until the gelatine has dissolved completely. Add some of the lemon mixture to the gelatine and then carefully fold both mixtures together. Whisk the egg whites until they form a stiff peak; set the soufflé mixture on ice. Just as the mixture begins to thicken, fold in the egg whites. Pour into the prepared soufflé bowl and put in a cool place to set for several hours.

When the soufflé is set, peel off the paper. Press the toasted nuts gently round the sides. Decorate the top with rosettes of cream and tiny sprigs of lemon balm or sweet geranium leaves.

Lime Soufflé

Serves 6–8

Follow the above recipe but use 3 limes. Decorate with very fine slices of lime which have been simmered in a sugar syrup until they are translucent.

Hot Lemon Soufflé

Serves 4–6

This is not a real soufflé in the generally accepted sense, but an old-fashioned family pudding which separates into two quite distinct layers when it cooks: it has a fluffy top and a creamy lemon base.

1 oz (30 g/¼ stick) butter
6 ozs (170 g/scant ¾ cup) castor
   sugar
2 ozs (55 g/scant ½ cup) flour

2 eggs (preferably free-range)
1 lemon
8 fl ozs (250 ml/1 cup) milk

Decoration
icing sugar

1 x 2 pint (1.1 L) capacity pie
   dish

Cream the butter well. Add the castor sugar and beat well. Grate the rind of the lemon and squeeze and strain its juice; separate the egg yolks and add one by one, then stir in the flour and gradually add the finely grated rind and juice of the lemon (see below). Lastly add the milk. Whisk the egg whites stiffly in a bowl and fold gently into the lemon mixture. Pour into a pie dish and bake in a moderate oven, 180°C/350°F/regulo 4, for 40 minutes approx. Dredge with icing sugar.

Serve immediately with softly whipped cream.

Note: If the lemons are very pale, use the zest of 1½ or 2 to give a sharper lemon flavour.

Apple and Sweet Geranium Compote

Serves 6

Use the scented geranium, *Pelargonium Graveolens*, to flavour this delicious Apple Compote—just a few leaves give it a haunting lemon flavour.

8 medium-sized eating apples,
   e.g. Golden Delicious
6 ozs (170 g/1 generous cup)
   sugar

juice of 1½ lemons
4 large, sweet geranium leaves
2–3 strips of lemon rind

Peel, quarter, core and slice the apples into $\frac{1}{4}$ inch (5 mm) segments. Put them into a stainless steel or enamel saucepan. Add the sugar, lemon rind and juice and sweet geranium leaves. Cover with a greaseproof paper lid and the lid of the saucepan; cook on a gentle heat until the apples are soft but not broken. They may be cooked in a moderate oven, 180°C/350°F/regulo 4, if that is more convenient.

Serve warm or cold with softly whipped cream.

Mangoes in Lime Syrup

Serves 2

This simple recipe must be made with a perfectly ripe mango; if the fruit you buy is under-ripe, wrap it in newspaper and keep it in your kitchen for a few days.

1 ripe mango	4 fl ozs (100 ml/$\frac{1}{2}$ cup) water
4 ozs (110 g/$\frac{1}{2}$ cup) sugar	1 lime

Put the sugar and water into a saucepan, stir over a gentle heat until the sugar dissolves, bring to the boil and simmer for 2 minutes; allow to cool.

Peel the mango and slice quite thinly down to the stone. Put the slices into a bowl and cover with the cold syrup.

Meanwhile remove the zest from the lime either with a zester or a fine stainless steel grater and add to the syrup with the juice of the lime. Leave to macerate for at least an hour. Serve chilled.

Note: Papayas are also delicious served in exactly the same way.

A Fruit Salad of Pink Grapefruit, Melon, Kiwi Fruit and Lime Juice

Serves 4

This is a very refreshing fruit salad, perfect to clear the palate after a rich meal.

1 pink grapefruit	1 lime
$\frac{1}{2}$ a ripe Ogen or Gallia melon	1–2 tablesp. castor sugar (taste
1–2 kiwi fruits	and use more if necessary)

Carefully segment the grapefruit into a white bowl. Scoop the melon into balls with a melon-baller and add into the bowl. Peel the kiwi fruit thinly and slice into $\frac{1}{4}$ inch (5 mm) slices. Juice the lime and pour it over the fruit. Add castor sugar to taste. Allow to macerate for at least 1 hour before serving.

Bananas with Lime and Orange Zest*

Serves 4

4 bananas	1 lime
4 ozs (110 g/$\frac{1}{2}$ cup) sugar	1 orange
7 fl ozs (200 ml/scant 1 cup) water	

Make a syrup by dissolving the sugar in 7 fl ozs (200 ml/scant 1 cup) water over a medium heat, then simmer for 2–3 minutes and allow to cool. Pare the zests from the lime and orange with a swivel-top peeler; cut them into the finest julienne strips. Put the strips into a saucepan of cold water, bring to the boil and simmer for 4–5 minutes. Drain and refresh with cold water and drain again.

Squeeze the juice from the lime and orange. Slice the bananas at an angle or into rounds. Add the bananas with the fruit juices and zests to the cold syrup, reserving a little zest for decoration. Pour into a pretty dish. Sprinkle the reserved zests on top and leave the fruit to macerate in a cool place for at least 2 hours. Serve chilled.

Green Gooseberry and Elderflower Compote

Serves 6–8

When I'm driving through country lanes in late May or early June, suddenly I spy the elderflower coming into blossom. Then I know it's time to go and search on gooseberry bushes for the hard, green fruit, far too under-ripe at that stage to eat raw, but wonderful cooked in tarts or fools or in this delicious Compote. Elderflowers have an extraordinary affinity with green gooseberries and by a happy arrangement of nature they are both in season at the same time.

2 lbs (900 g) green gooseberries	1 pint (600 ml/2$\frac{1}{2}$ cups) cold water
2 *or* 3 elderflower heads	1 lb (450 g/2 cups) sugar

First top and tail the gooseberries. Tie 2 or 3 elderflower heads in a little square of muslin, put in a stainless steel or enamelled saucepan, add the sugar and cover with cold water. Bring slowly to the boil and continue to boil for 2 minutes. Add the gooseberries and simmer just until the fruit bursts. Allow to get cold. Serve in a pretty bowl and decorate with fresh elderflowers.

Crème Caramel*

Serves 6

Caramel
8 ozs (225 g/1 cup) sugar
5 fl ozs (150 ml/generous $\frac{1}{2}$ cup)
 water

Caramel Sauce
2$\frac{1}{2}$ fl ozs (60 ml/generous $\frac{1}{4}$ cup)
 water

Custard
1 pint (600 ml/2$\frac{1}{2}$ cups) milk *or* **$\frac{1}{2}$**
 pint (300 ml/1$\frac{1}{4}$ cups) milk and
 $\frac{1}{2}$ pint (300 ml/1$\frac{1}{4}$ cups) cream
4 eggs (preferably free-range)

2 ozs (55 g/$\frac{1}{4}$ cup) castor sugar
vanilla pod *or* **$\frac{1}{2}$ teasp. pure**
 vanilla essence (optional)

1 x 5 inch (12.5 cm) charlotte
 mould *or* **6 x 3 inch (7.5 cm)**
 soufflé dishes

First make the caramel. Put the sugar and 5 fl ozs (150 ml/generous $\frac{1}{2}$ cup) water into a heavy-bottomed saucepan and stir over a gentle heat until the sugar is fully dissolved. Bring to the boil, remove the spoon and cook until the caramel becomes golden brown or what we call chestnut colour. Do not stir and do not shake the pan. If sugar crystals form around the side of the pan, brush them down with cold water. When the caramel is ready for lining the moulds, it must be used immediately or it will become hard and cold.

Coat the bottom of the charlotte mould or soufflé dishes with the hot caramel. Dilute the remainder of the caramel with 2$\frac{1}{2}$ fl ozs (60 ml/ generous $\frac{1}{4}$ cup) water, return to the heat to dissolve and keep aside to serve around the caramel custard.

Next make the custard. Whisk the eggs, castor sugar and vanilla essence (if used) until thoroughly mixed but not too fluffy. Alternatively, infuse the vanilla pod in the milk and cream; bring them to just under boiling point and pour onto the egg mixture, whisking gently as you pour. Strain and pour into the prepared moulds, filling them to the top. Place the moulds in a bain-marie of simmering water, cover with a paper lid and bake in a moderate oven, 180°C/350°F/regulo 4, 35 minutes approx. for individual dishes and 1 hour approx. for a charlotte mould. Test the custards by putting a skewer in the centre; it will come out clean when the custards are fully cooked.

Cool and turn out onto a round, flat dish or individual plates. Pour the remaining caramel around. Serve with a little softly whipped cream.

Caramel Mousse with Praline

Serves 6

$\frac{1}{2}$ lb (225 g/1 generous cup) castor sugar

4 fl ozs (100 ml/$\frac{1}{2}$ cup) water

4 egg yolks (preferably free-range)

2 level teasp. (1 American teasp.) gelatine

$\frac{1}{2}$ pint (300 ml/1$\frac{1}{4}$ cups) whipped cream

5 fl ozs (150 ml/generous $\frac{1}{2}$ cup) hot water

2 tablesp. ($\frac{1}{8}$ cup) water

Praline Decoration
1 oz (30 g) whole almonds, unskinned

1 oz (30 g) sugar

Put the castor sugar into a heavy-bottomed saucepan with the 4 fl ozs (100 ml/$\frac{1}{2}$ cup) water. Stir over a gentle heat until the sugar is dissolved and the water comes to the boil. Continue to boil until it turns a nice chestnut-brown colour. Remove from the heat and immediately add the 5 fl ozs (150 ml/generous $\frac{1}{2}$ cup) hot water. Return to a low heat and cook until the caramel thickens to a thick, syrupy texture, 3 or 4 minutes approx.

Meanwhile, whisk the egg yolks until fluffy, then pour the boiling caramel onto the egg yolks, whisking all the time until the mixture reaches the ribbon stage or will hold a figure of 8. Sponge the gelatine in the 2 tablespoons ($\frac{1}{8}$ cup) of water in a small bowl, then put the bowl into a saucepan of simmering water until the gelatine has completely dissolved. Stir a few spoonfuls of the mousse into the gelatine, then carefully add the mixture to the rest of the mousse. Fold in the cream gently and pour into a serving dish. Chill until set.

Decorate with rosettes of cream and crushed Praline.

To make Praline: Put the almonds and sugar into a small heavy-bottomed saucepan on a low heat. Do not stir. Gradually the sugar will melt and turn to caramel. When this happens, and not before, rotate the saucepan so that the caramel coats the almonds. By now the almonds should be popping. Turn onto a lightly oiled tin, allow to get cold and then crush to a rough powder.

Note: If you would like to make this into a caramel soufflé, fold in the stiffly beaten whites of 2 eggs after the cream. Chill until set and decorate as before.

Orange Caramel Cream

Serves 7–8

The recipe for this extremely rich and delicious orange-flavoured Caramel Cream was given to me by an Australian friend, Margaret Beard.

Caramel
4 ozs (110 g/½ cup) sugar
2½ fl ozs (60 ml/generous ¼ cup)
   water

Orange Custard
1 pint (600 ml/2½ cups) cream
2 oranges
3 eggs (preferably free-range)
4 egg yolks
4½ ozs (160 g/generous ½ cup)
   castor sugar

12 fl ozs (350 ml/1½ cups) fresh
   orange juice
2½ fl ozs (60 ml/generous ¼ cup)
   Grand Marnier

Garnish
orange segments
softly whipped cream

mint leaves

7 *or* 8 ramekins *or* soufflé dishes
   4 fl ozs (½ cup) capacity

First make the caramel. Put the sugar and water into a heavy-bottomed saucepan and stir over a gentle heat until the sugar is dissolved. Bring to the boil, remove the spoon and cook until the syrup turns to a caramel. Do not stir and do not shake the pan. If sugar crystals form around the sides of the pan, brush them down with cold water. When the caramel is chestnut-brown colour it is ready for lining moulds and it must be used immediately or it will become hard and cold. Coat the bottom of the soufflé dishes with the hot caramel and keep aside. Heat the cream to scalding point.

Grate the zest from 2 oranges on the finest part of a grater. Whisk the eggs and yolks in a bowl and add the castor sugar and zest. Whisk in the orange juice and Grand Marnier. Gradually pour in the hot cream, whisking constantly. Pour this custard mixture into the moulds. Place the ramekins in a bain-marie of simmering water. The water must only be hot, not boiling. A folded tea-towel under the ramekins in the water will help to keep the temperature down. Cover with a paper lid and bake for $1\frac{1}{2}$–2 hours in a low oven, 150°C/300°F/regulo 2.

Test the custards by putting a skewer into the centre; it will come out clean when the custards are fully cooked. Cool and chill. Unmould and garnish with orange segments and mint leaves. Serve with softly whipped cream.

Caramel Ice-cream with Caramel Sauce and Bananas

Serves 6–8

2 ozs (55 g/$\frac{1}{4}$ cup) sugar
4 fl ozs (120 ml/$\frac{1}{2}$ cup) cold water
4 fl ozs (120 ml/$\frac{1}{2}$ cup) hot water
2 egg yolks (preferably free-range)

$\frac{1}{2}$ teasp. pure vanilla essence
1 pint (600 ml/2$\frac{1}{2}$ cups) softly whipped cream

Put the egg yolks into a bowl and whisk until light and fluffy (keep the whites for meringues). Combine the sugar and 4 fl ozs (120 ml/$\frac{1}{2}$ cup) cold water in a small heavy-bottomed saucepan. Stir over a gentle heat until the sugar is completely dissolved, then remove the spoon and boil until the syrup caramelises to a dark rich chestnut-brown. Quickly pour on 4 fl ozs (120 ml/$\frac{1}{2}$cup) of hot water. Do not stir. Boil gently until it again becomes a smooth, thick syrup and reaches the 'thread' stage, 106°–113°C/223°–236°F. It will look thick and syrupy when a spoon is dipped in. Pour this boiling syrup onto the egg yolks. Add the vanilla essence and continue to whisk until it becomes a thick, creamy mousse.

Fold the softly whipped cream into the mousse, pour into a bowl, cover and freeze.

Caramel Sauce

8 ozs (225 g/1 generous cup) sugar

3 fl ozs (80 ml/⅓ cup) cold water

8 fl ozs (250 ml/1 cup) hot water

2 bananas

Dissolve the sugar in 3 fl ozs (80 ml/⅓ cup) of water over a gentle heat. Stir until all the sugar has dissolved, then remove the spoon and continue to simmer until the syrup caramelises to a pale-chestnut colour. If sugar crystals form during cooking, brush down the sides of the pan with a wet brush, but do not stir. Remove from the heat, pour in 8 fl ozs (250 ml/1 cup) hot water and continue to cook until the caramel dissolves and the sauce is quite smooth. Allow to get cold.

To serve: Scoop the ice-cream into a chilled bowl or ice bowl (*Simply Delicious*, pages 60–61). Slice the bananas at an angle and add to the sauce. Spoon over the ice-cream or serve separately.

Caramel Sauce keeps almost indefinitely in a glass jar in the fridge or any cold place.

Country Rhubarb Cake

Serves 8

This delicious Rhubarb Cake made from an enriched bread dough used to be made all over the country. Originally it would have been baked in a bastible or baker beside an open fire. My mother, who taught me this recipe, used to vary the filling with the seasons — from rhubarb to gooseberries, to damsons, blackberries and apples.

12 ozs (340 g/2½ cups) flour

2 ozs (55 g/¼ cup) castor sugar

a pinch of salt

½ teasp. bread soda

3 ozs (85 g/¾ stick) butter

1 egg (preferably free-range)

egg wash (see glossary)

5½ fl ozs (165 ml/¾ cup) buttermilk *or* sour milk

1½ lbs (675 g) rhubarb, finely chopped

6–8 ozs (170–225 g/¾ cup) granulated sugar

castor sugar for sprinkling

1 x 10 inch (25.5 cm) Pyrex *or* enamel plate

Preheat the oven to 180°C/350°F/regulo 4.

Sieve into a bowl the flour, castor sugar, salt and bread soda; rub in the butter. Whisk the egg and mix with the buttermilk. Make a well in the centre of the dry ingredients. Pour in most of the liquid and mix to a soft but not sticky dough; add the remainder of the liquid if necessary.

Sprinkle a little flour on the work surface, turn out the dough and pat gently into a round. Divide into two pieces: one should be slightly larger than the other; keep the larger one for the lid. Meanwhile dip your fingers in flour. Spread the smaller piece onto the plate. Scatter the finely chopped rhubarb all over the base, egg-wash the edges and sprinkle the rhubarb with sugar. Roll out the other piece of dough until it is exactly the size to cover the plate, lift it on and press gently to seal the edges. Make a hole in the centre for the steam to escape, egg-wash and sprinkle with a very small amount of sugar.

Bake in a moderate oven, 180°C/350°F/regulo 4, for 45 minutes to 1 hour or until the rhubarb is soft and the crust is golden. Leave it to sit for 15–20 minutes so that the juice can soak into the crust. Sprinkle with castor sugar. Serve still warm with a bowl of softly whipped cream and some moist, brown sugar.

Peter Lamb's Apple Charlotte

Serves 6–8

This is the scrummiest, most wickedly rich apple pudding ever. A friend, Peter Lamb, makes it as a special treat for me every now and then.

$1\frac{1}{2}$ lbs (675 g) apples (Cox's
   Orange Pippin are best but
   Bramley Seedling can be very
   good also)
$\frac{1}{2}$ oz (15 g/$\frac{1}{8}$ stick) butter
1 tablesp. water
4 ozs (110 g/$\frac{1}{2}$ cup) sugar
softly whipped cream to serve

1 loaf tin, 2 pints (1.1 L/3 cups)
   capacity

2 egg yolks (preferably
   free-range)
6 ozs (170 g/1$\frac{1}{2}$ sticks) butter
1 oz (30 g/$\frac{1}{8}$ cup) castor sugar
1 small loaf of good-quality
   white bread
1 egg white, lightly beaten

Peel and core the apples and cut into slices. Melt $\frac{1}{2}$ oz (15 g/$\frac{1}{8}$ stick) butter in a stainless steel saucepan with 1 tablespoon of water. Toss in the apples and 4 ozs (110 g/$\frac{1}{2}$ cup) sugar, cover and cook over a gentle heat until soft. Remove the lid if they are getting too juicy — you'll need a dry purée. Stir well, taste and add a little more sugar if necessary. Allow to cool for a few minutes and then beat in the egg yolks.

Meanwhile clarify the butter (see page 16).

Preheat the oven to 200°C/400°F/regulo 6.

Cut the crusts off the loaf and carefully cut the bread into thin slices, $\frac{1}{4}$ inch (5 mm) thick approx. Brush the tin with some butter and sprinkle with 1 oz (30 g/$\frac{1}{8}$ cup) approx. castor sugar. Cut 2 large pieces of bread, one to line the base of the tin and one for the top of the tin. Dip both sides of the bread into the melted butter. Line the base first, then line the sides of the tin. Cut the last of the bread into manageable-sized pieces, $1\frac{1}{2}$ inches (3.5 cm) wide approx., and line the sides with the buttery bread, making sure there are no gaps. Seal all the joins with lightly beaten egg whites. Fill the centre with the sweetened apple purée and put a lid of buttery bread on top. Bake in the preheated oven for 20 minutes approx. and then reduce the heat to 190°C/375°F/regulo 5 for a further 40 minutes approx. or until the bread is crisp and golden brown. Leave to settle for 10 minutes or so before turning it out of the tin.

Serve warm with a bowl of softly whipped cream — heavenly!

Notes

Notes

Notes

Notes

Notes